+F130 .P85 E85

F130 .P85 E85 C.1 STACKS 1978

F 130 P85 E85

Estades, Rosa.
Patterns of political participation of Puerto Ricans in New York City

DATE DUE

AUDREY COHEN COLLEGE LIBRARY
345 HUDSON STREET
NEW YORK, NY 10014

AUDREY COHEN COLLEGE LIBRARY
345 HUDSON STREET
NEW YORK, NY 10014

PATTERNS OF POLITICAL PARTICIPATION OF PUERTO RICANS IN NEW YORK CITY

SPANISH VERSION:
"PATRONES DE PARTICIPACION POLITICA
DE LOS PUERTORRIQUEÑOS EN LA CIUDAD
DE NUEVA YORK"

(Editorial Universitaria, 1978)

ROSA ESTADES

PATTERNS OF POLITICAL PARTICIPATION OF PUERTO RICANS IN NEW YORK CITY

EDITORIAL UNIVERSITARIA
UNIVERSIDAD DE PUERTO RICO
1978

FIRST EDITION, 1978

ALL RIGHTS RESERVED
© University of Puerto Rico, 1978

Library of Congress Cataloging in Publication Data
Estades, Rosa.
  Patterns of political participation of Puerto Ricans in New York City.
  Bibliography: p.
  Includes index.
  1. Puerto Ricans in New York (City) — Politics and government. 2. New York (City) — Politics and government—1951. 3. Political participation—New York (City). I. Title.
  F130. P85E85   320.9'747'104   77-11625   ISBN 0-8477-2445-X

Impreso en Puerto Rico por: Ramallo Bros. Printing, Inc., P. Duarte 227, Hato Rey, P. R.

TABLE OF CONTENTS

Chapter I	Introduction	1
	A. Research Problem	1
	B. Literature on Puerto Ricans	1
	C. Sociological Theory on Inmigration	7
	1. Social Organization	7
	2. Associational structures	10
	Footnotes	13
Chapter II	Political History of Puerto Rico	15
	The Spanish Domination	15
	The American Domination	17
	Puerto Rican Political Parties after 1898	19
	The Rise of the Popular Democratic Party	21
	Political Structure	25
	Footnotes	27
Chapter III	Transmission of Political Issues and Cultural Styles by Early Migrants 1917-1945	29
	Footnotes	36
Chapter IV	Patterns of Political Organization in the Post-War Period	37
	The Organization of the Community	38
	"Los Grupos de Compueblanos"	39
	The Desfile	39
	Political Representation	41
	Footnotes	44
Chapter V	New Styles of Political Action: Departures from Tradition	45
	Civil Rights	46
	Pickets to the **Daily News** and **New York** Magazine	47
	The Young Lords Party	48
	United Front Pro Puerto Rican Political Prisoners	50
	Footnotes	52

Chapter VI	Poverty Programs and Registration Drives as New Forms of Political Participation	53
	Population	53
	Segregation and Poverty Areas	54
	Poverty Programs	55
	From Clubhouses to Anti-Poverty Programs	56
	"La Cruzada Cívica del Voto"	58
	Footnotes	61
Chapter VII	The Puerto Ricans and Party Politics: Interlinks Between New York City and the Island	63
	The Democrats	63
	The Democratic Leader: Herman Badillo	65
	The Republicans	68
	The Liberals	69
	Footnotes	71
Chapter VIII	Puerto Ricans, Cubans and Dominicans: The Politics of Hispanismo	73
	Footnotes	78
Chapter IX	Findings and Conclusions	79
Appendix	Data and Field Work Procedure	88
Sources Consulted		92

CHAPTER I

INTRODUCTION

A. RESEARCH PROBLEM

This study is an attempt to describe how Puerto Ricans in New York City organize for political participation in their process of accommodation to New York City.
The following questions will be examined:

To what extent do Puerto Ricans follow the patterns of political participation that developed in Puerto Rico?
What new patterns have emerged in the process of their political activities in New York City?
What is the structure of the political institutions developed by Puerto Ricans in New York City?

The problem of this study is to examine how Puerto Ricans in New York City organize themselves politically. It relates Puerto Rican political institutions to forms of political expression in New York. It goes on to explore new forms of political institutions developed by Puerto Ricans in the City, including those that are based on reconnections with the Island because of participation in City Politics.

B. LITERATURE ON PUERTO RICANS

There is an abundance of literature on the migration of Puerto Ricans to the United States. The aspects of the organizational structures and of the political institutions and participation in politics, however, have been largely ignored. The problems studied in this literature have been those of demography, social maladjustment, impact on governmental services, and the role of the social and economic life in Puerto Rico in helping the receiving communities of New York to understand the migrants.

There have been six major studies published about the migration of Puerto Ricans and the life of the migrants in New York City. These studies have not focused on politics at the local level, but I have used their discussion of leadership and organization as my guidelines.

The first study was published in 1938 by the Columbia University Press. It was *The Puerto Rican Migrant in New York City*, a doctoral dissertation written by Lawrence Chenault, an economist who had worked in Puerto Rico. Chenault chose the topic because of his interest in the population problem of Puerto Rico. From him, as stated in his preface: "it was apparent that the migration of large numbers of Puerto Ricans to New York and other northern centers could easily have important and social consequences for these particular areas."[1] He gives three significant reasons for studying the problems: the expected acceleration of migration in the near future; the tendency of Puerto Ricans to settle in the Harlem section of New York City; and the recent agitation on the part of the Puerto Rican people for independence.

His book is divided into two parts: the first one: *Puerto Rico as a Source of Migration to the United States* and the second: *The Puerto Rican Worker and His Family in New York.* He makes clear that the discussion of the migrant in New York will be limited almost entirely to the families of the low income group which have moved to the Harlem settlement.

He estimates that one-half of all the Puerto Ricans living in the United States settle in the Harlem section. In 1930 there was no separate classification in the U.S. Census covering Puerto Rican people in the United States. We can only judge the total number of people of Puerto Rican origin by the number born in Puerto Rico living in the United States. Those of Puerto Rican parentage were not counted as Puerto Rican. According to the 1930 U.S. Census the estimated population of Puerto Ricans in the United States was 52,774. The estimate given by Chenault for 1935 was over 58,200. The New York City population of Puerto Ricans born in Puerto Rico in 1930 was 44,908; in 1935, 49,500; or approximately eighty five percent of the total Puerto Rican population in the United States.[2]

Chenault studied the areas of employment, housing, health, and the social adjustment of the migrant group. His chapter on "Social Adjustment in the New Community" is subdivided into a "Closer View of the Harlem Settlement of Puerto Ricans" (with an excellent description of the East Harlem settlement) and "Social Maladjustment — Crime and Delinquency in the Community." (This latter section included crime and delinquency among this group as well as in the community, disintegrating influences affecting the family, the need for vocational training, and the migrant's reaction to religious and political influences.)

Two pages of his study are dedicated to political influences affecting the migrant in Harlem and call attention to the parades and demonstrations which

> *In recent years have come to be almost a part of the life of the colony. Nationalist campaigns for independence in Puerto Rico have extended to the settlement in New York; organizations for independence have been formed and small contributions have been sent back to the Island for the cause. During recent trouble growing out of the independence movement on the Island, the sympathy of the group in New York was apparently entirely on the side of those favoring independence.*[3]

Mr. Chenault also mentions the sympathy of the majority of Puerto Ricans with the Loyalists in Spain. He says:

> *If there are any Fascist sympathizers, they are not in evidence at the demonstrations over this issue, so might this sympathy for the Loyalist be partly accounted for by the fact that many of the Puerto Ricans are Socialists. In regard to partisan affiliation, the Puerto Rican is almost without exception Democratic.*[4]

In spite of Chenault's perceptive analysis, his study never dealt at length with the aspects of organizations and leadership. His main concern was on the social impact of the migration, and he doesn't even suggest that the area of organizations and leadership is worthy of investigation. (He writes his study, of course, knowing fully the meager sources of information at that time and the lack of statistical and other reports.)

To this day, without doubt, Chenault is the main source of information on this period. All other observers have relied on him as the source and authority on the Puerto Rican migrant group in the thirties.

The Puerto Rican Journey, by C. W. Mills, Clarence Senior and Rose Goldsen, (New York, Harper, 1950), was the second study about migration. It is the most comprehensive research on the migration of Puerto Ricans, and was sponsored by Columbia University and the Government of Puerto Rico. The study is divided into three parts: The Island, The Journey, and The City. Without doubt it is the one most quoted, and twenty years after its publication there is no book as detailed in its analysis.

In Part Three, "The Puerto Rican World," the authors study the New York organizations. Their remarks are as follows:

> *Such organizations as do exist are few and weak. Several organizations exist in the city among people connected by having the same hometown in Puerto Rico, the same occupation in New York or some other such link. Some clubs have been in operation for over twenty years.*

They arrive at the conclusion that "it is clear that organizations of Puerto Rican character do not play any key role in the life of the migrant."[5]

In regard to voting they comment:

> *As Puerto Ricans become more settled residents they are drawn into political participation. In the absence of any community organizations of their own to help them when they are in trouble and to defend them in public, the machine of Congressman Vito Marcantonio function.*

They say in another paragraph on the same page:

> *"Mr. Marcantonio's influence, obviously, is not adversely affected by constant newspaper criticism of his friendship for the migrant."* [6]

According to them the Puerto Rican world is a fragmented, disunited sphere for social living without a wide network of organizations, without effective Puerto Rican leadership and with evidence of internal class splits within it.[7]

The Puerto Rican population in New York City, at the time their study was written, was estimated as 248,880 according to the 1950 census figures, the first census where Puerto Ricans were counted as such. In 1940, a census which also used the criteria of birth in Puerto Rico, there were 61,463. The annual influx after the war was over accelerated at a rapid rate from 29,500 in 1950, it reached a peak of 51,800 in 1953. These figures are of great importance as background to what Mills and associates were studying in their sample population. The large numbers of migrants were already of greater impact on the life of the city. Their dispersion to other areas and districts was also taking place.

The Newcomers, Negroes and Puerto Ricans in a Changing Metropolis by Oscar Handlin, (Harvard University Press. 1959), is one of a series of studies on the forces that shape urban areas, in this case the twenty-two counties of the New York Metropolitan area. The study was undertaken by the School of Public Administration at Harvard University for the Regional Plan Association, Inc. In his introduction, Handlin says:

> The method of this effort to comprehend the situation of present day New York ethnic groups will be largely historical. An examination of the population of the city in terms of its ethnic characteristics may isolate and define the problems involved in the adjustment of immigrants to urban life. [He adds]... the question will then be raised as to whether and how the Negroes and Puerto Ricans of the first three decades are significantly different from the immigrants of the first three hundred years of New York history.[8]

He hoped to trace a line of future development helpful to understanding the character of the community as a whole. Referring to the character of their communal organizations, he found the Negroes and Puerto Ricans to be the farthest removed from the experiences of earlier immigrants and that they have not developed the integrated pattern of voluntary organizations that gave their predecessors understanding of the problems of metropolitan life and aid in dealing with them. He finds it significant that the philanthropic institutions established and supported by the nineteenth century immigrants had no counterpart among the Negroes or Puerto Ricans. As a result, they could not find the help they needed within the context of the group, and the group lacked this means of giving its identity significant expression.

He continues his analysis of both groups and concludes that "giving due regard to what actually has developed, it is still true that the Negroes and Puerto Ricans have not matched the richness and health of the communal life of the earlier immigrants."[9] To him poverty alone is not enough to explain the difference; complex reasons generated a sense of apathy toward communal organizations that has played an important part in shaping the character of their adjustment, such as the "break" of migration, the difficulties of citizenship, the influence of mass media, the discouraging economy and the obligations assumed by the welfare state. He find both groups yielding readily to the tendency to turn from the responsibility of voluntary agencies to governmental agencies.

Another thoughtful book is Beyond the Melting Pot — The Negroes, Puerto Ricans, Jews, Italians and Irish of New York by Nathan Glazer and D. P. Moynihan. (Published by the Joint Center for Urban Studies, a cooperative venture of the Massachusetts Institute of Technology and Harvard University in 1963.)

In their study of Puerto Ricans, the portion written by Nathan Glazer attributes the closeness to the Island as a factor in the relative weakness of community organization and leadership. He analyzes this closeness as related to the differences in social classes among the migrants and the identification as Hispanos with other Spanish speaking groups on the basis of upper income and social status.

The authors found many social organizations among Puerto Ricans that were not as strong and closely knit, however, as the societies of the earlier immigrants. To them this was due to the growing dependence for recreation and entertainment on movies, television, and other commercialized recreation. The practical functions of voluntary associations for aiding the poor and sick are now in the hands of public and private agencies, instead of in the hands of Puerto Rican social organizations.

Their analysis of the postwar period is based on the conclusion of *The Puerto Rican Journey*. Chenault is the source for their brief mention of prewar migration. The relation to the Island as a factor affecting the organizational life of Puerto Ricans in New York City is mentioned in the role played by the Office of the Commonwealth of Puerto Rico and its offices throughout the mainland. They describe the functions of representation and the services rendered with the comment: "It may very well be that it is because the Puerto Rican group has been so well supplied with paternalistic guidance from their own government, as well as with social services by the city and private agencies, that it has not developed powerful grassroots organizations.[10]

In the introduction to the 1970's edition they found that Puerto Ricans are economically and occupationally worse off than Negroes, but with a substantial move upward in the second generation, as they had anticipated in the edition of 1963. Puerto Ricans ended the 1960's with less promise than any other group, and they

> "emerged from the decade as the group with the highest incidence of poverty and the lowest number of men of public position who bargain and broker the arrangements of the city. They had no elected officials, no prominent religious leaders, no writers, no powerful organizations."

According to them, in spite of all this powerlessness, Puerto Ricans show little despair and a good deal of hope, and to them this suggests that Puerto Ricans still see themselves in the immigrant ethnic model; that is, "they see their poor economic and political position as reflecting recency of arrival and evil circumstances that can still be overcome."[11]

A study by Elena Padilla, *Up From Puerto Rico*,* is valuable as background to the understanding of the factors of race, generation, class, religion, township and their resulting influence on the pattern of organization and the development of a criterion of differentiation from European immigrants.

Her analysis of cliques, the dyadic relationships and the role of the "building" leaders in the community are essential to understanding the life of

---

* *Up From Puerto Rico* by Elena Padilla, (Columbia University Press, New York, 1958)

the migrants. Her use of "hispano" as the term used by migrants to refer to themselves is of interest to the analysis undertaken in this study.

Another study by Joseph P. Fitzpatrick, *Puerto Rican Americans — The Meaning of Migration to the Mainland*,** sums up most of what social scientists have said about Puerto Ricans, plus Father Fitzpatrick's own observations and research over two decades. He deals with an overall assessment of the meaning of migration for Puerto Ricans as inheritors of the role of strangers in a strange land and their adjustment to the city. He goes beyond the context of the city's earlier history as melting pot to examine the new dimensions of both the city and the new migration. The focus of his study is the quest of the Puerto Ricans for identity in the "replaying of a familiar basic theme, but with a significant variation.:: The crucial point for him is the problem of what specific identity the Puerto Ricans will eventually have as they become New Yorkers, and what special problems they will face.

His interpretive effort takes him into a detailed analysis of the Island as the background to an understanding of the dynamics of migration, the consequent uprootedness and disorganization of the migrant's family, religion, problem of color, efforts at the organization of a community, the situation in the schools, and the special problems of mental illness and drug abuse. His emphasis, except for his chapter on community, is on social disorganization aspects accompanying the migration.

In his chapter on the Puerto Rican community in New York City, he examines the settlements since the twenties, the geographical dispersion after World War II, and the present political representation. He describes the organization of the Puerto Rican agencies in the City, highlighting the history and the role played by the office of the Commonwealth of Puerto Rico. He relies on secondary sources and on his own observations as an "involved participant" in the life of both Puerto Rico and New York City.

In his last chapter, dedicated to the meaning of migration, he states:

> It is doubtful that Puerto Ricans will achieve a deep sense of identity through the development of a strong community on the model of the earlier immigrant groups. In simple terms of residential settlement, the patterns of urban redevelopment and the public housing make it impossible for them to cluster in strong, tightly knit communities. The basis of this strength will have to be sought elsewhere. Related to this is the difficulty of establishing a strong community on the basis of religious identification with the Puerto Rican parish.[12]

He goes on to mention the proximity of the Island and the ease of return to promt the Puerto Ricans to find in the Island the sense of strength, support, and identity which former immigrants found in the clusters of their own kind in the immigrant communities of American cities. Language for Fitzpatrick does not seem to be a basis for identity at the present time.

** *Puerto Rican Americans — The Meaning of Migration to the Mainland* by Joseph P. Fitzpatrick, (Prentice Hall, New Jersey, 1971)

He finds the shift in emphasis from culture to power as the basis for community strategy and formation in the past fifteen years. "In this process, community strength comes to be promoted not only by an emphasis on the preservation of culture, but in the organizing of resources around community interest."[13]

He agrees with the theory of assimilation presented by Glazer and Moynihan, that the melting pot had never actually melted; instead of people defining their interest around nationality background they define them now around race or religion. For them: "the ethnic groups have become large scale interest groups. The United States faces the accommodation of conflicting interests in a politically unified society."[14]

In relation to the power movement as basis for organization and identification, Father Fitzpatrick states: "It is not yet clear what will become the basis of community strength which will enable Puerto Ricans to move securely and confidently into full participation in the city's life, and no particular theory of assimilation is adequate to analyze it."[15]

In his review of Father Fitzpatrick's book for the magazine, *America*, in the October 30, 1971 issue, Nathan Glazer arrives at the conclusion that "Puerto Ricans were unlucky enough to arrive on the mainland when New York City and the country was 'between models' for relating new groups to an old, mixed society. A split identity may be the result." Glazer examines in this article the three traditional models — "Americanization", "Assimilation" and "Melting Pot"; radical separation as experienced by the Negroes, Chinese, Japanese, and perhaps the Mexican-Americans, and in a modest way a good part of the Jewish community. The third model, the "ethnic model" where all the groups aspire to important elements of common status — political, economic, social — all wish to maintain some element of distinctiveness. According to Glazer, Puerto Ricans had the misfortune to arrive in New York City at a time when the third model was giving way to a new version of the second: when the battle for desegregation, integration and ultimate assimilation of Negroes was giving way to a new mood of group self-assertion and the questioning of the goals of desegregation, integration and assimilation — the "Black Power" movement. To Glazer, the pages dedicated to the analysis of what this has meant for Puerto Ricans is Father Fitzpatrick's greatest contribution.

In regard to partisan politics both Glazer and Fitzpatrick find Puerto Ricans committed to the Democratic Party. Commenting on the lack of political representation as of 1970, Fitzpatrick sounds a pessimistic note in his conclusion that "strong political action both proceeds from community strength and contributes to an increase of community strength."

C. SOCIOLOGICAL THEORY ON IMMIGRATION

1. Social Organization

In this study we are concerned with the social organization of the

Puerto Rican migrant community. Several studies of prior immigrant groups were particularly helpful in our analysis.

William I. Thomas and Florian Znaniecki in their classic *The Polish Peasant in Europe and America — Monograph of an Immigrant Group*, divide their study of the Polish-American community into what they call "the two most important aspects of the life of Polish immigrants — the formation of the Polish-American national society, and the individual disorganization resulting from the imperfect coherence of this society and its consequent partial failure to organize and control all the Polish immigrants in a manner sufficient to prevent the spread of moral decadence."[16] Their fifth volume is entitled *Organization and Disorganization in America*.

Of particular interest as a guideline for analysis of the problem of the present study is the portion devoted to the organization of the Polish-American community out of what they call "the originally incoherent elements." To them the most striking element in this process of community formation toward self-determination is found in the study of the political field.

In their analysis of the organization of the community they examine the role of the "society," and "association." These were established invariably whenever the colony reached 300 members and Florian and Znaniecki considered these as factors in the unification of the community. Through "super territorial"organizations the Polish-Americans tried to unify all of the Polish "societies." Whatever tendencies these associations had, one official purpose in common was the preservation of Polish ethnicity among their members. Since Poland was involved in its struggle for independence, these organizations subscribed to Polish patriotism as well as to meeting the many and practical interests connected with their immediate social environment. Their chief aim was "to preserve the cultural stock brought by the immigrants to America — language, mores, customs, historical tradition — so as to maintain the racial solidarity of the Poles as an ethnic group, independent of their political allegiance and of any economic, social, or political bonds which may connect each of them individually with their American milieu."[17]

According to Thomas and Znaniecki, the different political divisions among the Polish-Americans made it impossible to create a single organization embracing all local groups. These different political divisions had no connection with American politics; they were at the beginning imported from Europe, but slowly were "redefined under the influence of the internal social problems of Polish-American life."[18] They concluded that these struggles helped to form large numbers of American Poles into a self-conscious body working toward the solidarity of their immigrant community in America.

In studying how Puerto Ricans organize in New York City for political participation I found similarities between the Polish-Americans and the Puerto Ricans in their process of organization, such as: preservation of the culture of the homeland; transmission of values to the new community; and the question of "patriotism." Since neither Poland nor Puerto Rico are independent, many similar orientations exists. The solution to the political status of Puerto Rico has been central to the political organization and participation of Puerto Ricans, both in Puerto Rico and New York City.

Like the Poles, Puerto Ricans are also trying to unify the community and to organize for partisan political participation, trying to accommodate the different political factions that divide the community. These factions also originated in the homeland and were imported into the American experience.

The "redefinition of goals" described by Thomas and Znaniecki, which the Poles underwent under the pressures of adjustment to American life, slowly contributed to the solidarity of their immigrant community. In the Puerto Rican case a similar redefinition of goals occurred during the decade of the Sixties when official statistics revealed the Puerto Ricans as the poorest group in the City, and the group with the least political representation to represent the interests of the migrant community. The Puerto Rican migrants and their leadership realized that a fuller participation in their community and the life of the City was needed to be able to survive in a critical and difficult situation. The shifting from the "island-centered" interests to the migrants community in the City increased the solidarity of the group and motivated the group to organize politically to get a proportional share of funds from anti-poverty programs, and other Federal, State and City funds.

Some Poles could not adjust, and 15 to 20% of the emigrants returned to Poland. Similarly, after World War II, a larger percentage of Puerto Rican migrants went back to Puerto Rico. It was easier for them to return to their homeland than it had been for the Poles, because of political ties, distance, and ease of transportation.

By 1960, the movement of Puerto Ricans to New York City had dwindled to an annual total of about 15 to 20 thousand. According to the demographic studies of José Hernández Alvarez[*] a steadily increasing number of migrants returned to Puerto Rico, a reverse movement which cancels the net gain in the population on the mainland by way of migration.

This study of the Polish immigrant community highlighted the difference between what eventually happened to the Poles and what has happened to the Puerto Ricans in their process of community formation as examined in the historical periods of the Puerto Rican migration.

The inter-war migration period, 1917 to 1945, shows the greatest similarity between the community formation of the Polish-American and the Puerto Rican community. Chapter Three, an attempt at an historical reconstruction of the community of the early migrants, describes how these migrants transmitted their homeland cultural and political values to their first important settlement, East Harlem.

The differences between both groups gradually appear as the Puerto Rican community of the Fifties, the Post-War period, develops a pattern of dependency on the Island which was possible due to the political relationship of Puerto Rico and the United States. These reconnections and their impact

---

[*] Hernández Alvarez, Jose, *Return Migration to Puerto Rico.* (Population Monograph Series, No. 1. Berkeley, University of California. 1967) p.6.

on the organization for political participation are the greatest difference between the Poles and the Puerto Ricans.

With Poland attaining independence, the Poles suscribed and remained loyal to the culture and values of their homeland, but their main interest was the welfare and solidarity of their Polish-American community.

Puerto Rican migrants despite the shift in interest to their migrant community, because of the new patterns developed during the Fifties, of financial and leadership representation from the Island, have been unable to sever their ties with their homeland. These new patterns of dependency make the Puerto Rican migrant group different from the Poles, and from all other immigrant groups who came before.

2. Associational Structures

Lloyd Warner and Paul S. Lunt in their study, *The Social Life of a Modern Community* examine the associational structure of Yankee City. They postulated their first hypothesis on the behavior and function of associations "to integrate the larger inner structures of the society to the whole community... the association helps to resolve these antagonisms, at the same time it may also organize the antagonisms of the members of these structures against the larger community."[19]

They found associations in all groups in Yankee City, both among the Yankee and the ethnic groups. "Closed" associations were those whose membership was taken

> *from one ethnic group and concern themselves principally with the maintenance of the solidarity of the group; they keep alive the members' interest in the homeland, and help to adjust their relations to the Yankee City community which is new to them.*[20]

Despite the difference between the social structure of Yankee City, which Warner and Lunt considered as having a coherent social organization, and the social structure of New York City, which they described as having an incoherent social organization, their analysis of the associational structures was of particular applicability to the study of the Puerto Rican community social organization. Their criteria for classification of organizations, the concern of "closed associations" with the solidarity of the group, their interest in their homeland, and process of adjustment to the new community will help us in our analysis of the organization of the Puerto Rican community.

The present thesis suggests that in their process of political organization in the City, the Puerto Rican migrant community shares many of the experiences of prior immigrants. The group with whom they have the greatest similarity are the Poles, because of those factors already mentioned. The ethnic groups of Yankee City, as described by Warner and Lunt, also went through a similar process of the transmission of homeland cultural values, the resolutions of antagonisms against the structures of the overall society, and the adjustment to the receiving community.

10

Both Thomas and Znaniecki and Warner and Lunt, found similarities in the functions of "societies" and "associations". For Thomas and Znaniecki the "society" was a factor in the unification of the community and attempts were made to unify all societies into "super-territorial" organizations. Their official purpose was the preservation of their "ethnicity." Warner and Lunt found the "close-associations" of Yankee City concerning themselves with the maintenance of the solidarity of their ethnic community. Both studies analyze the concern of "societies" and "associations" with the resolution of factionalism and antagonism within the ethnic community, and acting as mechanisms of integration with the overall receiving communities. This holds true for the Puerto Rican community as well.

The uniqueness of the Puerto Rican experience appears to be the combination of these familiar patterns lived by other incoming "national" groups and the new patterns developed because of the political interconnections between the Island and the United States and the advanced state of technology of which the Puerto Rican migration took place. Therefore, the process of accommodation to life in the City and particularly to the political organization of the group will be shaped to a large extent by these new patterns in the Puerto Rican experience.

Since the purpose of this study is to examine the way in which Puerto Ricans in New York City organize for politcal participation, a search for historical perspectives and backgrounds takes us first to a consideration of the political history of the Island.

The first migration period, from 1917 to 1945, will be referred to as the Inter-War Migration Period. Beginning with the granting of U.S. citizenship to Puerto Ricans in 1917, this period continues to the end of World War II.

Migration after 1945, the Post War Period, was marked by an ingrease in migration, population dispersion, and closer connections with the Island for political purposes.

The cutoff point for this period is the election year of 1964, when the Republican Party won the mayoralty election in New York. Both Governor Muñoz Marín of Puerto Rico and Mayor Robert F. Wagner of New York were no longer in office. The result was that the political arrangements that had existed between the Island and the City were no longer operational. A new set of relationships had to be established.

Chapters Five and Six examine the decade of the Sixties, with its new forms of political participation and new political institutions.

The inter-links between the Island and New York City are examined in the analysis of participation in partisan politics, particularly in the 1972 mayoralty elections.

The politics of "hispanismo" are examined as a challenge to the solidarity of the hispanic world, and the efforts of the political leaders to deal with the situation.

In this examination of the formation of the Puerto Rican migrant community for participation in politics, this study goes beyond what the literature on the migrant community has so far studied. It examines the patterns of political participation of the migrants in Puerto Rico before they migrate and how these migrants transmit their values to their new community. No previous examination had been done by the students of the Puerto Rican migration of the political history of the Island as an essential background to the understanding of the values and patterns lived in Puerto Rico and transmitted to life in the City. The impact of the political interconnections between the Island and the United States in the formation of the Puerto Rican migrant community, particularly in the attempts at organization for participation in partisan politics has not been dealt with in any historical perspective.

No attempt previous to our own has been made at an historical reconstruction of the life and settlement of the early migrants and to compare this period, 1917 to 1945, with the Post-War period. The criteria for most studies have been the growth in numbers and dispersion and mobility without a due consideration of the United States society during the Inter-War period, particularly the life in New York City.

Since *The Puerto Rican Journey* by C. W. Mills, Clarence Senior and Associates was published in 1950, no large scale study has been attempted. Their conclusions are still valid, but the changes in this migrant community merits reconsideration of the problem as they studied it. The changes of the Fifties and Sixties have not been adequately studied until now.

No examination of the ideological cleavages due to the political relationship of the Island and the United States has been attempted before. This study examines in detail the factions and the cleavages, both those originating in the Island, and the new ones, such as the "hispanismo" versus "puertorriqueñismo" within the hispanic world of New York.

From this literature we, however, have taken as a point of departure Glazer's[*] theory that ethnic groups have become large-scale interest groups which confront the United States with the problem of accommodation of conflicting interests in a politically unified society. It explores what Fitzpatrick called the shift in emphasis from culture to power as the basis for community strategy and formation. The purpose of this study is to fill the gap in the literature of Puerto Rican migration by an in-depth examination of the community formation within an historical perspective.

---

[*] From Glazer's review of Father Joseph Fitzpatrick's book on Puerto Ricans in the magazine *America*, October 30, 1971 issue.

FOOTNOTES

1. Lawrence R. Chenault, *The Puerto Rican Migrant in New York City,* (Columbia University Press, 1938. Reissued 1970, by Russell and Russell), Preface, p. i.
2. Ibid., p.58.
3. Ibid., p.153.
4. Ibid., p.154.
5. C. Wright Mills, Clarence Senior, Rose Goldsen, *The Puerto Rican Journey,* (Harper and Brothers, 1950. Reissued, 1967, Russell and Russell) p.105.
6. Ibid., p.108.
7. Ibid., p.133.
8. Oscar Handlin, *The Newcomers, Negroes and Puerto Ricans in a Changing Metropolis,* (Harvard University Press, 1959.), p.3.
9. Ibid., p.109.
10. Nathan Glazer, Daniel P. Moynihan, *Beyond the Melting Pot,* (The MIT Press, Cambridge, 1963. Second Edition, 1970), p.110.
11. Ibid., p.XIX.
12. Joseph P. Fitzpatrick, *Puerto Rican Americans — The Meaning of Migration to the Mainland,* (Prentice Hall, New Jersey, 1971), p.179.
13. Ibid., p.181.
14. Ibid., p.181.
15. Ibid., p.184.
16. William I. Thomas, Florian Znaniecki, *The Polish Peasant in Europe and America — A Monograph of an Immigrant Group,* (The Gorham Press, Boston, 1920), Volume V, p.XVIII.
17. Ibid., p.98.
18. Ibid., p.110.
19. Lloyd Warner, Paul S. Lunt, *The Social Life of a Modern Community,* (Yale University Press, Yankee City Series — 1941), Volume K, p.302.
20. Ibid., p.305.

CHAPTER II

POLITICAL HISTORY OF PUERTO RICO

THE SPANISH DOMINATION

Puerto Rico's first three centuries have been called, perhaps ironically, by one of its writers as: "the period of formation and passive accumulation in the development of our nation, which starts with the discovery and conquests, and finishes at the end of the 18th Century and the beginnings of the 19th Century . . . when we were nothing but a faithful prolongation of the Spanish culture."[1]

Julian Steward and his group in their cultural historical approach to the study of contemporary Puerto Rico divided the first three centuries into two different periods: Period I, 1493-1700 — Discovery and Introduction of Iberian Patterns, and Period II, 1700-1815 — Increasing Export Agriculture.[2]

Most historians agree that the restrictive policies of the Spanish Crown inhibited the development of Puerto Rican agriculture and commerce and kept the Island in isolation from the main currents of social, economic and political thought of the rest of the Western World.

In the early 19th Century, the Crown lifted some of the severe restrictions which had been imposed on Puerto Rico and thus started the century which has been generally regarded as the century of the crystallization of a native Puerto Rican national consciousness. Starting in 1815 until 1898, this Period III of the Spanish Domination was marked by an expansion of commercial and economic activity, but also by political and social ferment.[3]

In 1493, aboriginal Puerto Rico was populated by Arawak Indians, who during the first period of colonization far outnumbered the white settlers. Conservative estimates set the figure at about 50,000. This native population decreased very rapidly and Negroes were imported and the institution of slavery was established early in the 16th Century.

In the late 18th Century and early 19th Century, the colonies of South America and the Caribbean pressured for political reforms or complete separation from the Crown. A Puerto Rican identity arose separating themselves from the new Spanish immigrants and from the elements in the population which remained loyal to the Crown. The latter were mostly the minority who ruled the Island's military and commercial affairs. This Puerto Rican identity manifested itself in different social and reform movements which already marked the future alignment in terms of political parties.[4]

The political activities of Puerto Ricans during the Spanish domination found expression in organized pressure groups rather than in avowed political parties. Already three distinct groups, corresponding to political and social ideologies, emerged: the Conservatives, Spanish Loyalists, interested in continuing cultural and political ties to Spain; the Liberals, who demanded reform and autonomy as part of the union with Spain; and the Separatists, who, embued with the spirit for freedom of the European and Latin American revolution, envisioned Puerto Rico as a Republic. Thus the three basic political forces, which to these days shape Puerto Rican partisan politics, emerged during the 19th Century: assimilationists, reformists or autonomists, and independents.

During the apogee of the Spanish Empire, the government of the colonies followed a more or less similar pattern, depending on the wealth and national resources, especially gold, found in each colony.

In Puerto Rico, during the 16th to the end of the 18th Century, government control of commerce was arbitrary in its administration and discouraging in its effect on the Island's insular economic development. Private property in land was legally established in 1778, giving rise to a class of wealthy farmers who could influence governmental policies.[5]

At this time the power to make decisions in Puerto Rico rested with the Crown — local interests of the Island were secondary to Spain. The Governor acted in the name of the Crown and symbolized power. The check on the Governor's power rested with the Church and the Council of the Indies, who could appeal directly to the Crown. Governors were removed if their policies displeased the Spanish Crown.

The Council of the Indies, organized in 1542, commanded a great deal of executive, legal, financial, police, military, religious, and commercial power. Its members were appointed by the King and had permanent session in Madrid.[6]

Puerto Rico was colonized by Catholics acting under the sovereignty of the Crown, where the function of the Church and State was closely linked. Puerto Rico continued to be almost completely Catholic until the American occupation in 1898. There was control by the Crown both of the Army and the Church, the two principal Spanish institutions on the Island. The unity of Church and State thus provided sacred validation of secular norms of social behavior.

During the 19th Century, when Spain was busy with Latin American rebellions and its overseas wars, the Governor of Puerto Rico continued to hold the power to retard or advance measures which could benefit the Island. He was charged with the maintenance of the system of defense and public order, headed the administrative apparatus of the Island, appointed the municipal mayors, and supervised the execution of laws. Periods of social and political pressures by Puerto Ricans were met either by repressive or conciliatory measures. As an example, in 1823, the Puerto Rican deputy to Spain presented a bill to the Spanish seeking more autonomy for the Antillean colonies, Cuba and Puerto Rico. Madrid responded in 1825 and was to subject the Island to perhaps its worst colonial period, for forty-two consecutive years, under fourteen Spanish military governors, who assumed absolute power and abolished the civil rights that Puerto Rican reformers had slowly and painfully extracted from the Crown. This parade of what historians have called, "Little Caesars" helped to increase the ferment on the Island, and a pattern of sporadic revolt, rebellion, and protest followed by sterner measures developed.[7]

There was growing pressure for abolition and equal rights for the Negro. In 1848, the Black code of General Prim was promulgated to discourage slave revolts, by adopting punitive measures for slaves who rebelled, including the death penalty, while a Free Negro bearing arms was subject only to maiming. The role of the Free Negroes was of importance in both the abolitionist and in the development of Puerto Rican national consciousness, joining ranks with the Puerto Ricans in an anti-Spanish sentiment. When slavery was abolished in the United States, it stimulated the abolitionist movement in Puerto Rico. In 1873, slavery was finally abolished in the Island — about 30,000 slaves were freed.[8]

In 1897 Spain recognized the danger of losing its remaining colonies, and granted the Autonomic Charter. The Charter included the election of voting delegates to both houses of the Spanish Cortes, the election of thirty five members of the Island's House of Representatives, and eight out of fifteen members of the Administrative Council (which was equivalent to a Senate). The Governor General, appointed by Spain, chose the other seven senators. The Governor could also suspend civil rights in emergencies. Puerto Rico's legislature could pass on all matters of importance for the Island, fix the budget, determine tariff and taxes, and accept or reject any commercial treaties concluded by Spain without local participation.[9] This government officially began to function in July, 1898. It was short-lived, however, because of the Spanish American War. On the 15th of July, 1898, General Nelson A. Miles landed in Puerto Rico, and the American occupation began. Puerto Rico was ceded to the United States in the Treaty of Paris on December 10, 1898.[10]

THE AMERICAN DOMINATION

It has taken many pages for historians and observers of the Puerto Rican situation to describe the reactions of Puerto Ricans to this historical moment; therefore, with varied points of view and opinions, ranging from a description of the cordiality of peasants who knew little about the United States but had no reasons to love the Spaniards; to those who analyzed the reaction of the autonomists who had, for the first time, extracted substantial reforms from Spain, to the cautious warnings of the separatists, who even though they had known exile abroad, were fearful of the expansionist policies of the United States.

The initial "trauma" of the physical presence of the Army was soon replaced by the reality of a military government imposed on Puerto Rico which lasted until 1900, when the Foraker Act went into effect.

This act made Puerto Ricans neither American citizens nor citizens of an independent nation. Power again would be centralized in a Presidential appointed Governor, an eleven-man Executive Council (a majority of Americans), thirty-five elected Puerto Ricans in the House of Representatives (laws subject to Congressional veto) and an elected Resident Commissioner, who had a voice and no vote in the U.S. House of Representatives.[11]

Puerto Ricans, culturally different from the American colonial power, with a different language and religion, started a new colonial relationship full of uncertainties and stunned by the treatment they were getting from the neighbors of the North.

The Americans responded to this situation with an Americanization policy bearing a very strong resemblance to the one used with the 19th Century European immigrants. The educational system would be the first frontier in this colonization. The language and culture of the dominant nation, it was expected, would soon assimilate in the new possession. Americans were new and inexperienced in the colonial business; Puerto Ricans had had four hundred years of it.[12]

The Jones Act, which President Wilson signed on March 2, 1917, proclaimed American citizenship; Puerto Ricans became automatically U.S. citizens unless they signed a document refusing it. Refusal deprived them of numerous civil rights to hold public office, making them aliens in their own country. Puerto Ricans were also subject to be drafted.[13] During World War I, a Puerto Rican regiment served in Panama.

Just as Puerto Rico had been a military outpost for the Spanish Empire, it continued as a strong military outpost for the United States in the Caribbean. The first three decades of American rule were marked by the conflict arising out of the subordination of Puerto Ricans to new masters, and to the process of Americanization. Parallel to these political situations, changes were occurring with great significance for the social structure of the Island, as new economic, political, and religious patterns were superimposed by the American occupation.

The total population of Puerto Rico increased from 155,406 in 1800 to 953,243 in 1899. The census data classified 64% as white, the balance intermediate and Negroes. There is a continuous trend to a white increase in Puerto Rican population through the 20th Century, so that by 1940 the proportion of the population classified as non-white dropped to 23.5.[14] This classification and the way in which Puerto Rico's people have culturally defined the concept of race is one of the areas of greatest strain between the Anglo dominated culture of the United States and the Puerto Rican, both in Puerto Rico and when they migrate and settle in the United States.

This population at the beginning of the century was predominantly rural. Most of the Negroes, after abolition, settled in the sugar cane areas of the coastal regions of the Island in a way marking the first internal migration of the Island. This internal migration of people from the mountain area to the coastal area was later accelerated by the changes in the internal economy of the Island. The coffee industry continued to hold its own in the world market until the American occupation forced Puerto Rico to comply with American tariffs (1901-1902) and coastwise shipping laws. These events re-established sugar cultivation as the principal industry of the Island. By 1930, 60% of all sugar cultivation on the Island was absentee-controlled with virtually all the control residing in the United States.[15]

Slowly Puerto Rico's economy was integrated with that of the United States.[16] These changes in the economy, population movement, and commerce did not stop the greatest economic problem which has saddled Puerto Rico from the very beginning of its history — that of being one of the most overpopulated and poorest nations in the world. This state of affairs was further complicated by the depression in the United States, making the thirties one of the most difficult decades in the life of the Island with great implications for the economy, political development, and the resultant increased migratory flow to the United States.

PUERTO RICAN POLITICAL PARTIES AFTER 1898

In spite of the military government established in 1898, the Puerto Rican political leaders started to reorganize their parties. The autonomist leader, Luis Muñoz Rivera, with his work destroyed, tried once more to work with the new system, founded the new Federal Party, advocating federal union with the United States and immediate reform leading to the establishment of a civil government which would liberalize the existing order. The former Puro Party, the conservative party, reorganized themselves into a Republican Party, which also advocated a civil government and eventual integration and assimilation into the body politic of the United States.[17]

In the municipal elections held in July, 1899, which lasted 100 days until January, 1900, Muñoz Rivera Federal Party won forty-two of the sixty-four towns, and the Republicans, the remainder.[18]

In November, 1900, new elections were held under the new civil government; the Republican Party, favored by the Americans in the government, won the elections, and this anexionist party stayed in power until 1904. The Federal Party, claiming fraud, dissolved themselves and in 1904 formed the Union Party. During twenty-years this autonomist and reformist party stayed in power. In 1910, Muñoz Rivera, after learning English, was elected Resident Commissioner to Washington to fight for liberalized reform and autonomy for Puerto Rico. He has been credited with influencing the granting by the United States of citizenship to the Island residents. He diez in 1916; the leadership fell into the hands of two leaders, Antonio R. Barceló, a believer in autonomy and José De Diego, a believer in independence.

In 1924, the Republicans and the Union Party merged into the Alianza de Puerto Rico, with a commitment to reforms; they differed as far as preference for solutions to the status question. The Union advocated autonomy and the Republicans annexation. They won the elections of 1924 and 1928, opposing a coalition of Socialists, a newly formed labor party, and discontented Republicans.[19]

In 1930, a Brookings Institute Report, directed by Victor S. Clark, former Education Commissioner of Puerto Rico under the military government, sought to study scientifically the Island's persistent economic difficulties so that a basis might be found for the inauguration of constructive innovations.[20] It recommended an extension to the Island of all Federal aid extended to the States. In 1934, Puerto Rico was transferred from the War Department to the Department of the Interior. The outcome of the transfer was the establishment of the Puerto Rico Emergency Relief Administration and the Chardon Plan, which contained the genesis of an industrialization plan. The basic economic revolution never materialized; however, what were laid were the foundations for the reform program after 1940 of the Popular Democratic Party.[21]

In 1930, Barceló reorganized his party into a Liberal Party, and in 1932 lost to the coalition of Republicans and Socialists. This coalition of the Republicans, conservatives and assimilationists with what had promised to be a radical socialist party is one of the anomalies of Puerto Rican politics during the thirties.

The Nationalist Party, which had always existed even though it had never participated in the electoral process, went to the polls in 1932, under the leadership of its foremost exponent, Pedro Albizu Campos. The Nationalist leader had travelled through Latin America for two years trying to win support for the cause of Independence for Puerto Rico. The party lost at the polls. Albizu and his followers shifted to a policy of violence against the existing Colonial order and the stage was set in Puerto Rican politics for a violent decade in which two ideologies confronted each other —reform and revolution.[22]

Even though the Coalition won the elections of both 1932 and 1936, their assimilationist tendencies could not match the political sentiments stirred by the two central currents of reform — liberalism and the brand of nationalism and outright confrontation politics preached by Albizu. Albizu's opinion of the electoral process was quoted in "El Mundo", Puerto Rico's principal newspaper, November 16, 1933 as: "The electoral struggle in a periodic farce to keep the Puerto Rican family divided."[23]

For the Nationalists there was no essential difference in the policy of the Republicans and the Democrats of the United States. Even though Puerto Rico was suffering from serious economic disorganization and poverty, which as we shall see, were not mitigated by "New Deal" measures extended to the Island, the political status of the Island continued to be the major electoral issue. The parties in power, a coalition of Socialists and Republicans, favored statehood, but there was growing antipathy toward the United States.[24]

The most comprehensive study of the New Deal in Puerto Rico marks the end of the experiment with the close of 1938, "after the New Deal has definitely lost its renovating drive on the island."[25] This same year, 1938, Luis Muñoz Marín, son of the late political leader, Luis Muñoz Rivera, founded the *Acción Social Independentista*, the forerunner of the Popular Democratic Party which won the election in 1940, staying in power for twenty-eight years (until 1968). Then the Statehood Party won, principally due to the split within the Party and the formation of a *Partido del Pueblo* by the political heir and Governor of Puerto Rico from 1964 to 1968, Roberto Sánchez Vilella. How Muñoz Marín organized his party and retained its control for three decades has been the greatest political influence on the history of political participation in Puerto Rico. During the decade of the forties, Albizu Campos and his nationalist ideology continuously challenged Muñoz and his social and economic platform.

The Popular platform stated that the status was not an issue until the economic problems were solved. This idea was also challenged from the other extreme of the political continuum, the Republicans who advocated a solution to the status question through statehood. Even though Muñoz claimed the status was not an issue, in 1952, Puerto Rico became a Commonwealth, which at the beginning was referred to as a temporary formula leading eventually to either independence or statehood. However, during later years commonwealth became the permanent formula advocated by his party as the ideal solution to the colonial dilemma of Puerto Rico.

THE RISE OF THE POPULAR DEMOCRATIC PARTY

Until the depression years, the problem of political status, with the three formulas for its solution, remained central to party politics in Puerto Rico. A series of circumstances made it possible at the end of the decade to witness the organization of a party with social and economic reforms as priorities in the party program, proclaiming at the same time that status was not an electoral issue. The possibility of such a reversal in Puerto Rican politics has been the subject of studies and opinions on the factors which made it possible.

Most observers agree on the importance of the founder and leader of the party, Luis Muñoz Marín. One of his biographers, Thomas Mathews, describes his background, American education, knowledge of English, and his friends and associates among the Washington New Dealers as factors which favored Muñoz in acquiring his leadership position, both in Puerto Rico and in Washington, and in organizing the party which could legislate into reality a social reform program equivalent to the New Deal to meet the needs of the Island. The Democratic administration and the incumbency of Roosevelt as President helped in the initial phases of the program.[26] From its beginning this party has always had close ties and affiliations with the Democratic Party of the United States.

On the Island, it helped the image of Muñoz as leader in the journalistic battles he waged against Governor Robert H. Gore in 1933. As it used to be the case with Spain it was with the United States regarding appointments for governors in the colonies. "President Franklin D. Roosevelt had little time for careful selection of candidates for minor appointments and this task was left to politicians. The man selected for the post was probably picked by James Farley from a long list of persons who expected appointments. Gore was a newspaper editor in a small midwestern state and a successful business man even during the depression. He lasted as Governor of Puerto Rico barely six months, and the man who brought him down was another newspaper editor, Luis Muñoz Marín."[27]

As related by Bolívar Pagán, in his "History of the Puerto Rican Political Parties," Muñoz's oratory and a new political style also helped in building up his image at some of the most critical moments at the beginning of his career. Muñoz used direct confrontation tactics with his political enemies when in the campaign of 1932 he was the target of a smear campaign because of his residence in Greenwich Village, New York, and his friends among the "intellectuals and bohemians."[28]

Muñoz had joined the Socialist Party during the twenties, and had campaigned throughout the Island as a Socialist*. This gave him a familiarity and a name with the masses of peasants who later, during the thirties, were betrayed by the Socialist leader Santiago Iglesias Pantín when they entered into a political pact with the Republicans, the conservative party with strong anti-labor feelings.[29]

Nowhere in available references is there an analysis of the impact of the granting of suffrage to women in Puerto Rico in 1932, nor of the ability of the leader to increase his constituency with women, whose low wages in the needle industry and their frustrations with the poverty and illnesses typical of such a depressed area made them ready for political involvement.

Party of the strategy of Muñoz and the Council of Founders in organizing the party was to reach the masses of Puerto Rico, the rural wage-earners and the small landowners who constituted the majority of the voting population since universal suffrage was a reality in Puerto Rico.

His political style and campaign tactics have been aptly described by many writers. Gordon Lewis refers to it in the following way:

> *The story of the genesis and organization of the new party in those two brief years (1938-1940) is nothing less than astonishing. It had to face and surmount the vulgar contempt of established parties... had to break away from the Puerto Rican habit of political leadership through family cliques in the deeply entrenched habits of electoral corruption, in particular the sales of votes for a small sum of money or a new pair of shoes... could not hope for the handsome donations from the sugar industry... the party's intellectual echelon of school and university teachers found that its members had to pay a harsh price, sometimes including dismissal from their posts, for their political affiliation.*[30]

This party, in its initial stages, sought not simply another reform brought from the outside. Their task was the changing of the whole colonial climate of thought by replacing the old social psychology of dependence on Spain and Washington and the apathy of the masses toward political participation, with a vigorous self-confidence within the individual Puerto Rican.

According to Gordon Lewis' analogies, the unique character of the campaign was first changing the party platform by avoiding the status issue, bringing the campaign to the majority element of the poverty-stricken agricultural workers and campaigning "throughout the length and breadth and in each tiny hamlet and barrio of the island."[31] The empty rhetoric foreign to the interest and life of the masses was changed to the use of indigenous words

---

* A non-Marxist, pro-labor party.

such as "el batey"*, "el machete", and the slogan "Pan, Tierra y Libertad."*
The flag bore the symbol of the "Jíbaro's pava" (peasant's hat). The *jíbaro*
has been regarded as the essence of the native culture and the symbol of Puerto
Rican identity.

The platform of the Popular party included measures of social and
economic reforms. The principal program was to be one of land reform. The
Foraker Act of 1900 had provided that corporate landholdings should be
limited to 500 acres, but this provision of the act had never been enforced.
The Popular party proposed to put teeth into the law.³²

The history of the way Muñoz and his party passed this legislation
which was signed by the last of the American Colonial government is much
too long to be included in this study. It was another gain for Puerto Rico that
Rexford Guy Tugwell was appointed Governor by Franklin D. Roosevelt. His
famous book describing his difficult time both in Puerto Rico and with his
enemies in Washington, "The Stricken Land" (1947) is an eloquent exposition
of the accomplishments of these two men.³³

In 1946, Jesús T. Piñero, the Popular Resident Commissioner to Washington was appointed by President Truman as the first Puerto Rican Governor.
The Puerto Ricans themselves elected their second governor, the President of
the Popular Party, Luis Muñoz Marín, in 1948. In 1952, after a referendum,
Puerto Ricans voted for a status of commonwealth realtion for Puerto Rico.³⁴

Changes on the position of the PPD* on the status question has been
characterized by some observers as the "gradual shifting... moving from a
thinly veiled independentism to an acceptance of the principle of permanent
association with the United States. Muñoz Marín's effective personal control
over the party and the pragmatic disposition of Puerto Rican parties have
allowed this transition to be carried out with a minimum of internal stress."³⁵

The "stresses" came particularly from the forces for independence with
particular strength during the thirties. In 1936, Colonel Riggs, the Island's police
chief was assassinated by two young nationalists who were, in turn, killed by the
police in the San Juan police headquarters.

The liberal American elements in Washington became very cool and
vindictive towards Muñoz, threatening the loss of all the gains he had made
with them, when he refused to condemn publicly Rigg's assassination unless
the American authorities condemned the killing of the two assassins. In 1937,
the tragic Ponce Massacre of Palm Sunday intensified the discontent. The
semi-militarized police fired upon an unarmed demonstration by the Nationalist Party. Twenty died, two of them policemen, and more than a hundred
were injured.

The Tydings Independence Bill was passed in 1936. It would have
spelled economic disaster and most of the political leaders in the Island
including the Republicans, were willing to accept it. The most significant

---
* "el batey" is front yard.
* "Pan, Tierra y Libertad" is Bread, Land and Freedom.
* PPD stands for Popular Democratic Party.

rejection to the Bill came from Muñoz Marín both in Washington and in Puerto Rico. When Muñoz founded his Popular Democratic Party, it had been commonly recognized that the leadership of the party favored independence. Muñoz himself, however, desired a continued legal and economic association with the United States.

In 1943, Senator Tydings was again responsible for introducing in Congress a bill to give Puerto Rico its independence. The PPD party platform contained a pledge to hold a plebiscite before any decision on the status would be taken.[36]

In January 1945, Senator Tydings once again introduced a bill giving independence to the Island. The *independentistas* drew up a list of amendments, most of which were incorporated into a separate independence bill presented in the House on March 26, 1945 by Congressman Vito Marcantonio, the political representative of the already growing Puerto Rican colony in the East Harlem area of New York.[37] The breach between the *Independentistas* within the Popular Party widened, and registration for a new party was begun in August; within four months the party had qualified in enough municipios to be included on the ballots through the Island for elections of 1948.

On October 30, 1950, the Nationalists revolted against the political order and tried to assassinate Muñoz. As a result, the Nationalist leaders were jailed, and the movement for independence was mainly continued by the *Independentistas*, who used the electoral process to seek a solution to the status question. Muñoz and the PPD continued on their political quest for a permanent commonwealth status, but the movement for independence continued as the ideology of those Puerto Ricans who see the solution of the Island's political status, rather than the solution of its economic problems, as the central and paramount issue in Puerto Rico.

The statehood movement, as represented in partisan politics by the Republican Party, resurged in 1968 as the *Partido Nuevo Progresista*, under the leadership of Luis A. Ferré. They defeated Muñoz's party in the election of 1968, claiming the status was not an issue, with the slogan: *"Esto tiene que cambiar"* ("This has to change").

As a result of the victory of the statehood party, the Island was polarized during the latter part of the sixties, and the status issue became once more the central focus of the political arena. The Independence Party became the *Partido Independentista Puertorriqueño* and a more militant faction previously known as the *Movimiento Pro Independencia*, with a Marxist Platform and with Cuba, Russia and Soviet leaning, became the *Partido Socialista Puertorriqueño*. The two leaders of these two parties, Professor Rubén Berríos denied tenure by the University of Puerto Rico, and chose to practice confrontation politics which brought him into conflict with the federal government in Puerto Rico and went to jail in 1970; and Juan Mari Bras, represent the separatist ideology, both with platforms calling for a Socialist Republic in Puerto Rico.

The elections of 1972 marked the return to power of the Populares. The pendulum apparently had swung from statehood to independence, but with a great majority at the polls, Puerto Ricans once more brought the center-autonomist leadership into power. Muñoz, who had been in political exile in Europe, came back to Puerto Rico shortly before the elections; his return was celebrated by a triumphant meeting of the *Populares*. This has been described by many as one of the factors for their victory.

POLITICAL STRUCTURE

Puerto Rico's government is highly centralized with most of the decision-making for internal matters of the Island taking place in the capital. The central authority figure is the governor; since 1946, a Puerto Rican occupies this position. But Puerto Ricans elect a governor whose decisions may be reversed by the President of the United States; the decision of their courts may be overruled by the Supreme Court of the United States, and Congress is the ultimate legislative power in those matters included in the Federal Relations Law of 1952. Even though the commonwealth status gave Puerto Rico more home rule, Puerto Rican leaders must still be bargainers and mediators of a dependent political status. Puerto Rican leaders must deal with a developing, rapidly industrializing society enmeshed in rapid social change while at the same time they must negotiate and deal with the politics of Washington.

Part of this process of negotiating, lobbying, and bargaining occurs around the realities of the massive migration of Puerto Ricans to the United States.

The Island is administratively divided into 80 *municipios* or municipalities, almost entirely subordinated to the central insular government. Each municipality elects a mayor and a municipal assembly, which includes representatives of the *barrios*, or wards, the smallest political unit. However, *barrios* have great significance as socio-cultural units. They tend to have cultural homogeneity resulting in most of the cases in uniform political outlooks.

Political loyalties are determined by many local factors. In rural situations, where there is a face-to-face relationship, a paternalistic relationship may overlap with the employers, landowners, who are usually members of a political apparatus. Family loyalties still operate in this region, descendants following their parents in political affiliation. The unions increasingly play a role in partisan loyalties.[38] This situation is changing with the increase in urbanization.

The internal structure of the major political parties tend to parallel that of the governmental organization. In his study of the Puerto Rican parties, Robert Anderson found that the Commonwealth Constitution "treats parties almost exclusively as nominating and electoral agencies, as adjuncts of the 'formal' government. All laws encourage cohesion, discipline and central control within the parties."[39]

In his chapter, devoted to the PPD, Anderson subtitles it as "The Politics of Personalism." He goes on to say:

The single most significant fact about the Popular Party is its almost total identification with the person of its founder and leader, Luis Muñoz Marín. The history of the party and of its ideological shifts and transformations is largely the history of Muñoz's own development and changing attitudes."[40]

Bolívar Pagán, historican and politician, former chairman of the now defunct Socialist Party, also characterizes, and throughout his two volume history, repeatedly alludes to: "... a tendency in Puerto Rico for the masses, once politically organized, to follow their leader."[41]

Religion has also played a key role in Puerto Rican politics — to the point that in the elections of 1960 a Christian Action party was hastily organized by the Catholic bishops, and polled 10% or more of the vote in 22 municipalities, 7% of the total Island-wide vote, Muñoz himself with his fine poetic intuition into the mind of the masses had used this cultural tradition of Puerto Ricans when he issued "The People's Catechism," written, like a platform with questions and answers spelling the ideology of his party to the masses.

Even by rigorous standards of political organization, the Puerto Rican political parties are too dependent on paternalism, and their centralization demands loyalty to the leader and to the party program. Puerto Rican parties are institutionalized structures which have effectively represented the main political ideologies of the Puerto Rican people and have involved, increasingly so, all social classes in the political process.

The new Electoral Code established in 1974 is a step towards the democratization, increasing participation and decentralization of the power of the political parties. The change brought about by this Code in the attitude of migrants towards political authority will probably be seen in their future political participation.

When they migrated to New York City Puerto Ricans brought their patterns of political participation with them. These patterns are characterized by many things: personalism, party loyalty, dependence on a centralized authority in both party and governmental structure, the desire for a solution to the political status question central to partisan politics, and the willingness to accept a reform program, if proposed by a strong political leader. These patterns give the political campaigns a personalistic character, with issues close to the lives of citizens and colorful and intense political campaigning.

During the inter-war period (1917-1945) these early migrants carried over their beliefs in the Island's political issues and in its cultural style as a part of their life in the City of New York.

FOOTNOTES

1. Antonio S. Pedreira, *Insularismo,* Biblioteca de Autores Puertorriqueños (San Juan, Puerto Rico, 1957), p.15.
2. Julian Steward, and Associates *The People of Puerto Rico* (University of Illinois Press, Urban, 1956), p.31.
3. Manuel Maldonado Denis, *A Socio-Historic Interpretation* (Vintage Books, New York, 1972.), p.23.
4. Ibid., Chapter 5.
5. Julian Steward, *The People of Puerto Rico,* p.59.
6. Gordon K. Lewis, *Puerto Rico Freedom and Power in the Caribbean* (Harper Torch Books, N.Y., 1963),Chapter 2.
7. Jose Luis Vivas, *Historia de Puerto Rico* (Las Americas Publishing Co., N.Y. 1962), p.143.
8. Luis Díaz-Soler, *Historia de la Esclavitud Negra en Puerto Rico, 1493-1890* (Ediciones de la Universidad de Puerto Rico, Rio Piedras, 1953), Chapter 9.
9. *Documents on the Constitutional History of Puerto Rico,* (Office of the Commonwealth of Puerto Rico, Washington, D.C. 1964), p.22.
10. Ibid., *Treaty of Paris* 1898, p.47.
11. Ibid., *First Organic Act of Puerto Rico,* 1900, p.64.
12. G. L. Osuna, *Education in Puerto Rico* (Teachers College Columbia University, N.Y. 1949) [The best description of the policies of the Governors of Puerto Rico regarding the teaching of English in Puerto Rico].
13. *Documents on the Constitutional History of Puerto Rico,* op. cit., p.41.
14. Julian Steward and Associates, *The People of Puerto Rico,* op. cit., p.41.
15. Bailey W. Diffie, and S. W. Diffie, *Porto Rico — A Broken Pledge* (The Vanguard Press, N.Y. 1931) p.135.
16. Julian Steward and Associates, op. cit., p.62-64.
17. José Luis Vivas, *Historia de Puerto Rico,* op. cit., p.184.
18. Ibid, p.184.
19. Bolívar Pagán, *Historia de los Partidos Políticos Puertorriqueños* (Librería Campos, San Juan, Puerto Rico, 1959), Vol. I.
20. Victor S. Clark and Associates, *Porto Rico and Its Problems,* (Brookings Institute, Washington, D.C. 1930), p.xxvii.
21. Gordon K. Lewis, op. cit., p.70.
22. Manuel Maldonado Denis, *Puerto Rico: A Socio Historic Interpretation.* op. cit., p.119.
23. Ibid, p.122.
24. Julian Steward and Associates. op. cit., p.80.
25. Thomas Mathews, *Puerto Rican Politics and The New Deal* (University of Florida Press, Gainesville, 1960), p.xi.
26. Thomas Mathews, *Luis Muñoz Marín — A Concise Biography.* (Institute of Caribbean Studies Editions — Roberta Strauss Feuerbacht American R.D.M. Corp., New York, 1967).
27. Ibid., p.23.
28. Bolívar Pagán, *Historia de los Partidos Políticos Puertorriqueños* (Librería Campos, San Juan, Puerto Rico, 1959) Vol. II, op. cit., p.42.
29. Thomas Mathews, op. cit., p.9.
30. Lewis, op. cit., p.90.
31. Ibid., p. 92.
32. Robert Anderson, *Party Politics in Puerto Rico.* (Stanford University Press, Stanford, 1965), pp. 68-72.
33. [The controversial administration of Tugwell in Puerto Rico has been the subject of numerous articles, comments and studies. Among the studies:

    Enrique Lugo Silva, *The Tugwell Administration in Puerto Rico —*

1941-46. (University of Puerto Rico Press, Rio Piedras, 1955).
Charles I. Goodsell, *Administration of a Revolution* (Harvard University Press, Boston, Mass. 1965)
34. Documents on the Constitutional History of Puerto Rico, op. cit., pp.113, 153, 168 (Elective Governor, *Public Law 66,* and *Constitution of the Commonwealth of Puerto Rico,* respectively.)
35. Robert Anderson, op. cit., p.49.
36. Ibid., p.110.
37. [Vito Marcantonio introduced several bills for the independence of Puerto Rico. The first bill was introduced in 1936. He presented it in the course of a debate on a Senate bill which he characterized as "the Tydings Bill for Fictitious Independence."] (See Rubenstein, Annette and Associates. *I Vote My Conscience — Debates, Speeches and Writings of Vito Marcantonio.* (The Marcantonio Memorial, New York, 1956. *Puerto Rico and the Puerto Rican People, 1935-1950,* pp.374-393.
38. Steward, op. cit., p.83.
39. Anderson, op. cit., p.18.
40. Ibid., p.76.
41. Bolívar Pagán, *Historia de los Partidos Políticos Puertorriqueños,* Vol. II, p.1.

CHAPTER III

TRANSMISSION OF POLITICAL ISSUES AND CULTURAL STYLES BY EARLY MIGRANTS —1917-1945

Puerto Rican migrants to New York City, unlike immigrants of the past, could register and vote upon acquiring residency. During the first migration period, the chief obstacle to exercising their rights at the polls was the literacy test they had to take requiring a knowledge of reading and writing in English. Until this test was eliminated, this was one of the chief obstacles on the path of the organization of their political structures.

Those who were literate and were politically inclined were quickly involved by leaders of their own ethnic group or by the politicians who represented the districts where Puerto Ricans settled in their early years in the city.

The Puerto Rican population during the thirties, when the first study was published, was estimated at close to 50,000 in 1935, with 80% of this population concentrated in the lower and eastern sections of Harlem. Other areas of concentration were in Brooklyn, along the waterfront from the Navy Yard south to Gowanus Canal. The west side of Manhattan and some areas north of Morningside Park going as far as and south of Washington Heights, also contained smaller settlements, as did Lower Manhattan and the South Bronx.[1]

Lawrence Chenault in his study *The Puerto Rican Migrant in New York City* locates the largest concentration at about 115th Street or 116th Street in East Harlem, an area which contained almost all the important institutions and places of business which served the Puerto Rican people in New York.[2] The area was also the center for parades and for the social and political activities of the community. He describes the political leadership as follows:

> Politically, the Puerto Ricans are now combined with other groups under a leadership which is not Puerto Rican. These political leaders in the Harlem district have gained influence with the group by declaring their sympathy for the movement for Puerto Rican independence, condemning the treatment of the island by the United States and constantly pressing for more liberal aid for the distressed people living in the Harlem area.[3]

Chenault is obviously alluding to Representative Vito Marcantonio, who represented the 17th Congressional district of Harlem, where the largest concentration of Puerto Ricans was found. The migrants knew about Marcantonio before they left Puerto Rico. He introduced the first bill for the independence of Puerto Rico on May 6, 1936. He denounced in Congress the large sugar industries on the island. Following is a quotation of Marcantonio's 1936 statement in Congress:

> Four large American sugar corporations own over half the good sugar land and produce over half the total crop... The landless peasants have been converted into a great army of colonial slaves in the sugar plantations, or are unemployed.[4]

As early as 1939 Marcantonio was protesting in Congress about the unjust way in which Puerto Rican children, because of the I.Q. ratings, were tested. He went to Puerto Rico after the March 1937 Ponce Massacre and on the floor of Congress denounced the police killings and Governor Blanton Winship's administration. He denounced the trials of the Nationalists in Puerto Rico, the jury selection, and how the Governor and Judge Snyder in Puerto Rico assured Washington of the conviction of the Nationalists who were later jailed in Atlanta.[5]

In his observations on the political life of the migrants, Chenault quotes *The New York Times* of August 30, 1936, describing the role of Marcantonio's after a two-week visit by the Congressman to the Island, "in spurring" ten thousand Puerto Ricans to denounce the attitude and actions of Americans in Puerto Rico.[6]

Even though Chenault's study was primarily concerned with the economic aspects of the migration, since Chenault was an economist who had worked in Puerto Rico, he gives this as one of the reasons for the importance of studying the Puerto Rican migration:

> So long as the island remains a territory of the United States, Puerto Ricans will, as citizens, be free to enter the United States without restriction. Undoubtedly the question of restriction of immigration from Puerto Rico would arise if complete independence were granted.[7]

Chenault grasped the significance of the status issue as a factor in the political organization in Puerto Rico and in New York City. He went on to say, later in his study:

> Nationalist campaigns for independence in Puerto Rico have extended to the settlement in New York, and organizations for independence have been formed and small contributions are sent back to the island for the cause. During the recent trouble growing out of the independence New York was apparently entirely on the side of those favoring independence.[8]

Another issue which was hotly discussed during the thirties among the Puerto Ricans and other Spanish speaking people was the Spanish Civil War. Chenault adds:

> Although a majority of the Puerto Ricans are professed Catholics, they are, as has already been brought out, almost invariably in sympathy with the Loyalists of Spain. If there are any Fascist sympathizers, they are not in evidence at the demonstrations over this issue. When the Spanish rebels bombarded Madrid in the summer of 1936, the Puerto Rican group took an active part in the parade of protest in which several thousand children in

the Harlem section marched... as in the case of the worker's attitude toward strikes, so might this sympathy for the Loyalist cause be partly accounted for by the fact that many of the Puerto Ricans are socialists.[9]

In my interviews with some of the migrants who came during the late twenties and during the thirties, two facts were found. Puerto Ricans still followed the issues and political life of Spain very closely since many had relatives in Spain caught in the struggle. Puerto Ricans had been influenced by the ideology of the pro-labor Socialist party. During the early period of its history as a party, Socialism, as preached by its founder, Santiago Iglesias Pantín, a Spaniard who had been jailed by the Spaniards because of his socialist ideas, had taken hold of the minds of the Puerto Rican workers, professionals, and intellectuals. Their attitudes during the thirties reflected the world-wide confrontation of ideas of right and left. The Spanish Civil War shows how, in this case, a brand of anti-clericalism had also influenced many Puerto Ricans, reflecting the schism of the Spanish struggle.

Parallel to these outside ideological involvements, there was a trend toward participation in the more liberal political parties of the City. In this respect, Chenault, describing the political preferences of the migrants during the thirties, says:

> Between the two major political parties, the Puerto Rican is almost without exception Democrat. It was during the administration of Wilson that the citizenship measure was passed; in 1928, the Democratic party platform contained a declaration favoring Puerto Rico's admission as a State.[10]

Here again, Chenault considers that whatever solution was favored, the status was an important factor in this period in the partisan political preference of the migrants.

From 1934 until 1945, Fiorello La Guardia, who had been a Congressman representing East Harlem since 1923-33, was the Mayor of New York. La Guardia was a Fusion candidate. His major opposition – the Democratic Party – had been shattered by the Seabury Investigation exposures and by its stubborn hostility to Roosevelt. The Republican leaders had no great strength with which to oppose him, and later the leaders of the American Labor Party were poorly organized and relatively unskilled in bargaining with so experienced a strategist and tactician as La Guardia. As chief of the Fusion party, La Guardia had a complex and contradictory role. His public posture was one of hostility to party, party leaders and party organizations; offstage, he was compelled, as is any Mayor, to lead his party or to be the prisoner of its leaders. He chose to lead.[11]

La Guardia was ranked by Wallace Sayre, author of *Governing New York City*, as the first among the eleven Mayors who have completed their terms in the office (Wagner, still in office, excluded.)"[12]

La Guardia was aware of the newest of the new immigrants – the Puerto Ricans. According to Arthur Mann, his biographer, on December 7, 1927, he wrote to E. F. Ramos, who santed his help to run for political office. "Could you send me a list of the Puerto Rican organizations located in my Congressional District? " Ramos answered: "There are no organizations, propaganda could be effective in restaurants, barber shops and cigar stores in which Puerto Ricans congregate."[13]

On March 17, 1928, before becoming Mayor, La Guardia introduced a bill in Congress, on Ramos's advice, requiring the Governor of Puerto Rico to be a native-born citizen of the Island and to be elected every four years. The bill failed to pass. He objected to the corporate holdings in Puerto Rico. However, La Guardia failed to organize Puerto Ricans in his district, and may have thus cost him the election of 1932. La Guardia disapproved of the movement for independence, and maintained that the problems were economic and that a Puerto Rican commonwealth status would profit from the free tariff policy.[14]

In 1937, the first Puerto Rican (representing East Harlem) was elected to the New York State Assembly. He was the late Oscar García Rivera, a lawyer by training and a Republican. In 1938, he ran with the American Labor party; next year he was defeated during a Roosevelt landslide.

In a personal interview I had with his widow, Dr. Eloísa García Rivera, she described the role of the migrants and the organizations of East Harlem for a political campaign as a very active enterprise closely resembling the political campaigns in the barrios of Puerto Rico. A great deal of cultural-ethnic pride was exhibited and loyalty to the candidates; his wife, claims that even though he belonged to the Republican party, his legislation was the kind of social reform corresponding more to a Socialist ideology than to a conservative stance. This she accounts for partly by his dissatisfaction with the Republican Party, and his decision to run with the American Labor Party, from which he seceded later on because of the leftist ideology of the party.

The Democratic Party also sought the votes of the migrants. Their leader, a Puerto Rican, was Dr. José N. Cesteros, an active social and political leader in the Puerto Rican and Spanish American community. According to "oldtimers" reports, Dr. Cesteros assumed leadership during the depression years, on behalf of the Spanish speaking community. His name appears on the letterhead of the Emergency Unemployment Relief Committee, South Harlem Committee headquarters, located at 1400 Fifth Avenue. The chairman of this committee was Harvey D. Gibson; Vice-chairman, Bayard F. Pope. The membership of the executive committee members representing a cross section of the leadership of the Puerto Rican and Spanish community.[15]

Through the aid of committees such as this one, and other civic activities, Dr. Cesteros was able to mobilize support for the Democrats. He was appointed Chairman of the Puerto Rican Division of the Democratic National Committee. By 1936, Dr. Cesteros had organized a fullfledged Division with the Hon. Robert F. Wagner, U.S. Senator from New York; Dennis Chávez, U.S. Senator from New Mexico; and Representative Adolph J. Sabath from Illinois as honorary members; 13 coordinators from New York City; 150 Advisory Committee members, and 27 members of a Ladies Committee. The majority of these were Puerto Ricans and some of these members are still active in Puerto Rican affairs and political life.

The group organized by Dr. Cesteros was instrumental in the Democratic National Campaign Committee to re-elect Roosevelt, working in cooperation with the Foreign Language Division of the National Democratic Party.

In June 1938 this group and a few other leaders formed a Puerto Rican Committee within the city-wide Independent Citizens Committee for the Election of Herbert H. Lehman and Charles Poletti for Congress. Dr. Cesteros organized the Puerto Rican Division Committee with coordinators for Upper Manhattan, Lower Manhattan, Washington Heights, Brooklyn, Queens, Richmond and The Bronx.

With the beginning of World War II the energies of the Community were directed toward the defense effort, and a committee was organized to write to the Puerto Rican soldiers from New York and Puerto Rico who were serving in the U.S. Army.

Reports of this period are contradictory and meager, since this phase of migration has been ignored in the history and study of migration. Historical reconstruction is needed to further analyze the social and political organization of this group of migrants.

Starting in the twenties, Puerto Ricans began organizing themselves in cultural, civic and social clubs. The leaders of these clubs were also active in politics and were sought after by the city's political and civic leaders as contacts with the newest migrant community. As a result of my personal interviews with leaders and from the records of "Revista Artes y Letras," edited by Doña Josefina Silva de Cintrón for twelve consecutive years (1933-1945) (See Table page 34), the following organizations listed and reported their activities chronicled during these years.

As described in my taped interviews and recorded in the two bound volumes of this journal, a picture of a socially and culturally active community emerges. These organizations had their own stationery and were mostly financed by their own members. Except for a very few who met in hotel suites, most of the organizers met in the living rooms of members.

These organizations were predominantly Puerto Rican: however, other Spanish Americans were also members. The group was finding familiarity and communalism on the basis of culture and language with other groups of Spanish speaking immigrants, especially mainland Spaniards and Cubans.

This group constituted on the whole a social, cultural and professional elite, but due to the homogeneity of the group and the geographical concentrations within the City, they were in close contact with the largest bulk of the migration, the workers and the less privileged migrants.

In the Puerto Rican community of today many of the high positions in government and membership on boards in associations of city-wide scope are occupied by some of the leaders who started out within their ethnically enclosed organizations during the thirties.

TABLE I

Organization	Year of Organization	Purpose
Club Videro	1920-22	Social & Political
Nueva York Sporting Club	1924	Social & Sports
Hermandad Puertorriqueña	1926	Benevolent & Charity
Club Esperanza	1926	Orientation for new migrants
Liga Puertorriqueña Hispana Eugenio María de Hostos	1928	Cultural
Círculo Cultural Cervantes	1930	Theatrical Presentations
Club Latino Americano	1930	Cultural & Social
Pan American Women's Assoc.	1930	Social & Cultural, Spanish and American Women
Club Caridad Humanitaria	1930	Women's Charity Club
Comisión Pro Centenario de Hostos	1939	Cultural
Misión Episcopal Hispana- Women's Auxiliary Group	1930	Charity
Sociedad de Mujeres Puertorriqueñas	1930	Civic & Cultural
Asociación de Empleados Civiles de Correo (P.R. Civil Service Assoc.)	1935	Civil & Social
Spanish Assoc. for the Blind	1935	Charity
Emergency Unemployment Relief Committee; South Harlem Committee Headquarters	1932	Welfare & Civic
Club Artes y Letras	1940	Cultural & Literary
Comité Hispano-Americano Pro Defensa de América	1941-45	Civic & Patriotic
Spanish Correspondence Pro Soldiers	1941-45	Civic & Patriotic

A copy of these two volumes is available at the New York City Public Library — Central Branch. (Revistas Artes y Letras)

This situation continued until the end of World War II, when with the economic expansion and greater ease of transportation migration steadily increased.

For close to three decades the early migrants had the opportunity of developing their first ethnic settlement in East Harlem. They transmitted their culture to the settlement and called it "El Barrio".

Even though the political issues and the cultural styles were patterned after the experience of the migrants on the Island, they did not show a patterns of dependency on Puerto Rico for the financing of their political endeavors. This group did their own bargaining for their political situation with the New York City political leaders.

During the postwar period, as migration continued to increase, government and private leaders of New York City and Puerto Rico looked for an improvement in cooperation and communication and for a program which would create significant changes in the life and political participation of the migrants.

FOOTNOTES

1. Lawrence R. Chenault, *The Puerto Rican Migrant in New York City*, (Columbia University Press, New York, 1938. Re-issued Russell & Russell, New Jersey, 1970.), pp.91-97.
2. Ibid., p.128.
3. Ibid., p.155.
4. Annette T. Rubenstein, and Associates, *I Vote My Conscience — Debates, Speeches and Writings of Vito Marcantonio, 1935-1950* (The Vito Marcantonio Memorial, 1956.), p.376.
5. Ibid., pp.390-391.
6. Chenault, op. cit., p.153.
7. Ibid., p.5.
8. Ibid., p.153.
9. Ibid., p.154.
10. Ibid., p.155.
11. Wallace S. Sayre and Herbert Kaufman, *Governing New York City*, (Russell Sage Foundation, N.Y. 1960), p.691.
12. Ibid., p.690.
13. Arthur Mann, *La Guardia — A Fighter Against His Times, Vol. I 1882-1933*. (J. B. Lippincott, N.Y. 1959), P.246.
14. Ibid., p.247.
15. Stationery copies and documents made available from the personal collection of documents of Doña Josefina S. Cintrón.

CHAPTER IV

PATTERNS OF POLITICAL ORGANIZATION IN THE POSTWAR PERIOD

Migration from Puerto Rico to New York City increased as soon as the war was ended and planes were available for the transporting of the migrants. At the end of the war, some of the war surplus planes were sold to private owners, and many Puerto Ricans came in chartered planes, newly converted to carry passengers. The sea transportation continued, but it diminished when air transportation became less costly. Some 200,000 Puerto Ricans lived in New York City in 1948.[1] Even though there were new areas of settlement such as in the Chelsea area of Manhattan, and several neighborhoods along Second Avenue, the blocks in Spanish Harlem and Morrisania constituted the core areas of settlement for the migrants.[2]

The volume of the migration increased during the fifties. Following are the yearly estimates of arrivals from Puerto Rico during the decade:[3]

Puerto Rican Migration to New York City[4]

Year	Estimated Migration to New York City
1950	29,500
1951	42,300
1952	45,500
1953	51,800
1954	16,100
1955	31,800
1956	34,000
1957	22,600
1958	17,000
1959	18,000
1960	9,600

The census of 1960 estimated the Puerto Rican population at 612,000. As of January, 1964, the Migration Division estimated a population of 702,886. This figure was based on average increases by birth since 1960 plus the percentage of the net migration that was estimated to remain in the city.

The extensive urban renewal programs and the construction of public middle income and luxury apartment buildings dislocated many neighborhoods in the city. This resulted in a dispersion of the Puerto Rican population, with a resultant pattern of movement within the city which was to affect the character of the settlements, the political representation of the community, and the entire life style of the migrants.

Father Joseph Fitzpatrick, an observer and analyst of this migration, describing the spread of the migration, writes:

> ... it is doubtful whether they have established those geographical concentrations which were so important to the strong communities of earlier immigrants.... One key to the strength of the earlier immigrants was the pattern of housing. At the point of second settlement, the earlier immigrants began to establish their tightly knit, strong communities.... They became stable, settled communities where a particular style of life was established and maintained.[5]

One example of how urban renewal affected the concentration of Puerto Ricans is the Lincoln Center area, where 7,500 families, more than half of them Puerto Ricans, resided on priceless urban land. Some of the Puerto Rican organizations established their headquarters in this area, and their members and leaders resided there. Some of these families were relocated in Rockaway Beach, where the possibilities of either belonging to or organizing a group were remote. If the leaders wished to look for membership in organizations they would have to start from the beginning. As we shall see, many of them did.[6]

Parallel to these two processes (increase in size and geographical dispersion) going on simultaneously within the community, a third was significantly shaping its life. This was the social and neighborhood organization.

THE ORGANIZATION OF THE COMMUNITY

Many of the new groups and organizations followed the pattern of those organized during the interwar period, dedicating themselves to social functions, and particularly to cultural affairs. The desire to preserve the culture of Puerot Rico was a goal of many of these new organizations.

Among them, an important one, founded in 1946, was the Institute of Puerto Rico. It was founded by Dr. Eloísa Rivera de García, the wife of the first Puerto Rican assemblyman, and by a group of professors and Puerto Rican intellectuals. This group is still active, pursuing the goals they outlined for themselves when they started. Journalists, writers, actors, teachers, and many other vocational interest-groups and professionals started to organize. The groups proliferated, some of them with a high mortality rate in membership and existence, but they somehow reorganized themselves and started to form the core of the leadership which was to assume representation on behalf of the migrant community. There was an increasing demand from each community for spokesmen for the migrants. The process, started during the Interwar period, continued at an accelerated pace.

LOS GRUPOS DE COMPUEBLANOS
(Hometown Groups)

The greatest single innovation in the pattern of organization of the community appeared during the fifties. Even though prior to the fifties two or three groups had organized themselves on the basis of place of birth, *municipio* or town, they had remained inactive and isolated until the new forces shaping the community, with the help received from the government of Puerto Rico agency, Migration Division, organized to aid the migrants in New York.

It was a very rapid movement and the groups modeled themselves on the pioneer groups. The principal incentives were to obtain a charter of organization, print letterheads, and then take an annual trip to their hometowns in Puerto Rico, and invite the Mayor and some other dignitaries to come to New York for affairs and banquets for the furthering of their organization. (The ultimate goal was to help those who came from the same "pueblo" and eventually send help for a worthy cause in their Island hometown.)

As a further incentive, the annual Puerto Rican parade was started. Each Island town wished to send its mayor and its beauty queen to parade proudly up Fifth Avenue. Seventy-seven *pueblos* were organized and later formed the Council of Hometown Groups, the organization which collectively assumed representation on behalf of all the groups.

The pattern of federation and councils of organizations appeared. Borough-wide councils subdivided themselves into neighborhood councils, for example, The Council of Lower East Side Puerto Rican Organizations.

Sports organizations also sprang up all over the city, especially baseball clubs, the favorite Puerto Rican sport. Las Ligas (leagues) incorporated the "little leagues". Youngsters who got uniforms with their names on them also participated annually in the *Desfile*.

The leaders of these new groups and federations were more interested in partisan politics than the leaders of the civic and cultural organizations. They were aware of their potential for power within the community and the large number of members they represented. During their trip to Puerto Rico and in the organization of the *Desfile* they made valuable political contacts both in New York and in Puerto Rico. They were hampered in their political ambitions by the lack of financial resources, since their members were mostly poor. However, during this decade the migrant community had laid the groundwork for the organizations that during the sixties would quickly take advantage of the resources provided by the community activities of the Anti-Poverty Program.

The Desfile

The first *Desfile* was Hispanic; Puerto Ricans participated but were not the organizers. As the Puerto Rican community organized itself, the leaders seceded from the *Desfile Hispano* and formed their own *Desfile*. The backbone of the *Desfile* were the hometown groups, with the Puerto Rican mayors, the Governor, and city dignitaries in the reviewing stand, or as participants in the *Desfile* itself. It has grown over the years and today it is a complicated activity, which marks the highlight of the life of the community. This is a predominantly grassroots movement; it is a day for "el pueblo" even though most Puerto Ricans belonging to all social classes participate and follow its progress.

Politicians, more than any other group, have profited from the *Desfile*. The Mayor of New York, with an eye on the increasing number of Puerto Ricans registering to vote, proclaims a week of June every year as Puerto Rican week, and makes the formal proclamation with good press coverage at City Hall. The annual banquet of the *Desfile* is increasingly a political banquet, where Puerto Ricans and city-wide politicians make their appearances to please their constituencies.

During the fifties the administration of New York was Democratic. Mayor Robert F. Wagner remained in City Hall for three consecutive administrations. In Puerto Rico the Popular Democratic Party kept winning elections and electing Muñoz Marín as their governor. Both Wagner and Muñoz stayed in power until 1964. (Muñoz's party retained power in 1964, but Roberto Sánchez Vilella was the political heir of the governorship).

During the fifties, a very close relationship was established between the Wagner and Muñoz administrations, and both parties — the Democrats of New York City and the *Populares* in Puerto Rico — profited from it. Mayors, and especially the Mayoress of San Juan, Doña Felisa Rincón de Gautier, were familiar figures campaigning during election years for the democratic candidates in New York City, especially in the Puerto Rican areas.

Migration conferences were held during these years; government officials from the City met either in Puerto Rico or in New York City to discuss programs and policies that would bring betterment to the needy Puerto Ricans who increasingly joined the ranks of the poor, unemployed and underemployed of the City.

The Migration Division of the Commonwealth of Puerto Rico has been praised by the community and its friends and observers, but a great deal of conflict has developed about the proper role this agency should play. As some Puerto Rican agencies developed they resented the principal role of the Division and their leaders wanted to assume the role of spokesmen for the community, claiming that their role was co-opted by the government agency. Even though the role of this Division has changed since the Poverty programs started in the sixties, the fact that some segments of the community still depend on its services results in an ambivalent attitude towards it.

Nathan Glazer, writing in 1963, says:

> There are probably many and subtle ways in which the relation of the island affects the organization life of Puerto Ricans in New York, but one clear impact is seen in the role of the Office of the Commonwealth of

Puerto Rico . . . but it is again a special twist for New York's Puerto Ricans that its equivalent of NAACP and National Urban League, or of the Jewish community organizational complex, should be a government office supported by government funds . . . it may very well be that it is because the Puerto Rican group has been so well supplied with paternalistic guidance from their own government, as well as with social services by city and private agencies, taht it has not developed powerful grassroots organizations.[7]

An evaluation of the role of this office is beyond the scope of this study, but the argument still goes on as I write, and no satisfactory solution to this dilemma is in sight.

POLITICAL REPRESENTATION

The organization of the migrant community into groups, federations, councils, parades and participation in conferences has not been accompanied by an equal success in political participation and representation. The requirement of having to take a literacy test in English to be able to register and vote continued to be a hindrance until it was ruled out by the Civil Rights Act of 1965. Lack of familiarity with what appeared to be a complicated voting machine kept some from casting their vote. During the primaries, many Puerto Rican voters do not vote. In spite of the fact that there is a primary law in Puerto Rico, the primary system is not used by most of the parties.

Since the enactment of the new Electoral Code in 1974 primaries are compulsory for all political parties, for all elective positions where more than one candidate aspires to nomination.

In New York the population dispersion has made it difficult for Puerto Ricans to penetrate the districts, and the mobility of the population within the city has prevented many from familiarizing themselves with the political and social institutions of their neighborhoods. The situation in the fifties and well into the end of the sixties looked very bleak for Puerto Rican political representation and power.

William O'Dwyer, the Democratic Mayor elected in 1946, took the first step on behalf of the Puerto Rican community by creating the "Mayor's Committee on Puerto Rican Affairs" six weeks before the mayoralty election of 1949. According to Dan Wakefield this was "evidence of the Mayor's vital interest in the Spanish-speaking peoples of the city, who potentially make up the fourth largest "national" bloc, behind the Italians, Irish and Jews."[8]

The Mayor's Committee was also continued by the administration of Vincent Impelliteri in 1950 and by Robert F. Wagner, until it was replaced by the Committee on Inter-Group Relations. The Inter-Group Relations committee, according to many Puerto Ricans, has never served the interests of the Puerto Rican community.

In their study of the Puerto Rican community of Spanish Harlem and Morrisania, Mills and associates, writing about the political participation of the migrants, say:

> *Less than half of the Puerto Ricans have at any time taken advantage of their voting privileges in the city... in view of the highly political atmosphere of the Island, the recent migrants' tendency to refrain from political activity in New York deserves discussion. Some 71 percent of the eligible voters exercised their vote on the Island in 1948, whereas 45 percent did so on the continent. From one interviewee they got the following comment: 'On the Island you grow up with the political issues, they are part of your life. In New York I don't even know who the candidates are, or what they are arguing about.*[9]

They found that in the absence of any community organizations of their own,

> *"to help them when they are in trouble, and to defend them in public, the machine of Congressman Vito Marcantonio functions. This machine carried on in the manner of the old style boss, has been highly successful in filling the lack of facilities among and for the migrants.*[10]

In 1951, Mayor Vincent Impelliteri appointed Emilio Núñez, who was of Spanish background but not a Puerto Rican, to the post of Special Sessions Justice. That was the last "Puerto Rican appointment" until 1957, when Mayor Wagner appointed the Puerto Rican, Manuel Gómez, as a judge.

In 1953, Ed Flynn, boss of the Bronx County Democratic Party, chose Felipe N. Torres as a candidate for Assemblyman from the Morrisania-Mott Haven section of The Bronx. With the support of the Flynn Club, he won and held his seat until he was later appointed judge.

The first acknowledgment of Puerto Ricans in Spanish Harlem occurred in 1954. Carmine De Sapio, Tammany Hall boss, appointed Antonio Méndez as the first Puerto Rican leader in the 14th Assembly District and thus came into being the Caribe Democratic Club and the first Puerto Rican district leader under the aegis of the regular machinery of the Democratic Party.[11]

Glazer, writing in 1963, found Puerto Ricans still committed to the Democrats. Analyzing the dilemma of ethnic groups and their relationship to the Democartic Party, a dilemma which he calls the "split personality" of the Jews, Italians, and Irish regarding the Democratic Party politics in New York City, he found the Negroes and Puerto Ricans "following the path of other immigrant groups solidly committed to the Democrats, both locally and nationally."[12]

In spite of the immigrant's almost total commitment to the Democratic Party, the Republicans have always been represented by a group of leaders who loyally adhered to their party principles. They kept themselves politically alive through participation in community activities voicing frequently "the loyal opposition" point of view. With the victory of Rockefeller as Governor of New York State this group found support and patronage from the State. These old-timers formed the Society Pro Statehood for Puerto Rico, which reflects their preference regarding the solution to the political status of the Island.

In the mayoralty elections of 1964, John V. Lindsay, a Republican, was elected Mayor of New York City. In Puerto Rico, although the *Populares* won, a new governor, Roberto Sánchez Vilella came into power. The old party alliances of the Muñoz-Wagner administrations ceased to exist. New leaders both in New York and in Puerto Rico, with new ideas about the government of the city, assumed the leadership role. The war on Poverty and its precursor in New York City — Mobilization for Youth on the Lower East Side, were also pointing to new developments in the nation and the city. The civil rights movement steadily changed its course from a passive to a more aggressive, militant and sometimes violent stance.

    The Puerto Ricans found themselves in the midst of a historic change in the life of the nation. Their social and political structures would be shaped to a large extent by all these new events. A new era had begun.

FOOTNOTES

1. C. Wright Mills and others. *The Puerto Rican Journey.* (Harper and Brothers, New York, 1950) p.22
2. Ibid., p.VII.
3. *A Summary of Facts and Figures.* (Migration Division of the Commonwealth of Puerto Rico, 1964-65 edition) p.16.
4. Ibid., p.17.
5. Joseph P. Fitzpatrick. *Puerto Rican Americans — The Meaning of Migration to the Mainland*, (Prentice Hall, Inc. Englewood Cliffs, New Jersey, 1971) p.57.
6. In the late fifties and early fifties and early sixties, I worked as a community organizer with the office of the Commonwealth of Puerto Rico. The office was located in the Lincoln Center area and ran a Housing Clinic to help migrants and other poor in the area with their housing problems.
7. Nathan Glazer, Daniel Moynihan, *Beyond the Melting Pot.* (The MIT Press, Cambridge, Mass., 1963) pp.108-110.
8. Dan Wakefield, *Island in The City*, (Houghton Mifflin Company, Boston, 1959) p.264.
9. C. Wright Mills and others, op.cit., p.108.
10. Ibid., p.109.
11. *El Diario de Nueva York*, March 12, 1973.
12. Nathan Glazer, op. cit., p.166.

CHAPTER V

NEW STYLES OF POLITICAL ACTION: DEPARTURES FROM TRADITION

The Puerto Rican community of the fifties and early sixties was described as an island-centered community by Glazer when he wrote his article in 1963 for the book *Beyond the Melting Pot*.[1]

Another characteristic of the Puerto Ricans at this time was a relative isolation from the life of the overall community. The migrants possessed an internal dynamic of intense leadership competition and factionalism. The less successful they were in terms of social and political recognition by the government and civil leaders, the more they turned their frustrations inward, into the busy life of the community.

A great deal of their hostility was discharged against what, in the eyes of the community, was the principal cause of everything that went wrong — the office of the Commonwealth of Puerto Rico, and particularly its director, Joseph Monserrat who during those years occupied the outstanding leadership position *vis-a-vis* the Puerto Ricans in New York City, the city officials, and the government of Puerto Rico.

As the community started to develop its own agencies to serve and represent the Puerto Rican migrants, a great deal of conflict accompanied the process. Perhaps the greatest conflict was the organization of the first agency financed by the Office of Economic Opportunity, the Puerto Rican Community Development Project. The struggle and factionalism was studied as part of Gotsch's master thesis for New York University, "Puerto Rican Leadership in New York", and also by Father Fitzpatrick in his chapter on the Puerto Rican community, in his book *The Puerto Rican Americans*.[2]

As the poverty program developed during the latter part of the sixties, the Puerto Ricans slowly realized that the pattern of communication of the minorities with the power structure had changed, and the civil rights movement of the Blacks had changed its national tactics to a more militant brand of protest. Consciousness of their lack of political power and their internal strife and fragmentation delayed the adoption by Puerto Ricans of this particular pattern, which to many migrants during those years appeared as tactics not suited to "the immigrant model" they had adopted for the community. However, as the funds were allocated and positions were assigned, the strife broke out in two new directions: one, at City Hall, where they accused Mayor Lindsay of lack of interest in the Puerto Rican community, and two, the Council on Poverty, which they charged was dominated by the Blacks.

During the first two years of his administration, Lindsay failed to communicate with the Puerto Rican leadership. He called a meeting at City Hall and invited about thirty leaders; over sixty leaders showed up. In a fit of temper, the Mayor violated some of the norms of Puerto Rican culture by showing amazement and lack of flexibility in not being able to handle the situation. The Spanish press criticized him severely, and he decided to take another step to establish communication.

He asked his community development staff and Marta Valle, the staff's highest level appointee, to organize a conference and get recommendations from the participants as to how the city could help solve the problems of the migrant community.

The conference was held on April 15 and 16, 1967. The conference recommendations and proceedings constitute a document or blue print for action on methods of dealing with the urban problems of the Puerto Ricans.[3]

Even though there were several followñup meetings with city officials, the rising expectations of Puerto Ricans were not even minimally met. Lindsay was severely criticized by the Black politicians and the conference organizers and was chastised by the Rev. Carl MacCall, of the Council on Poverty, who at one of the follow-up meetings told Puerto Ricans they should not have held the conference without including the Black leadership.

The summer of 1967 was marked by riots in many cities; in East Harlem Puerto Ricans rioted for days in what was to be the first of a series of new approaches in dealing with their plight in the city.

Puerto Ricans adopted the tactic of sit-ins, or office occupations, demonstrations which were characteristic of the protest movements of the sixties. As the city polarized towards the end of the sixties and early seventies, the migrants found themselves in many poverty areas of the city competing with the Blacks and other groups for control of community corporations, of local school boards, and of political district leadership.[4]

Whether they were successful or not is still very hard to tell, and in our examination of partisan political participation, we shall see to what extent the poverty programs helped Puerto Ricans to set up structures to enable them to compete with other groups. In dealing with some of the critical issues and situations of the community, the style had definitely changed. Following are some examples:

CIVIL RIGHTS

Puerto Ricans had followed the path of other groups in organizing themselves to protect their civil rights. They organized in the early sixties a National Puerto Rican Association for Civil Rights which followed the traditional approach of statements in hearings, annual meetings, and occasional representations as spokesmen for the community in city, state and federal functions.

On February 14th, 1972, the United States Civil Rights Commission conducted hearings to hear statements on the discrimination against Puerto Ricans in employment, housing, education, and other areas of their civil life. The Chairman of the Commission was Father Theodore M. Hesburgh, President of Notre Dame University. The hearings were interrupted by dissident Puerto Rican groups, forcing the Commission to adjourn. According to reports in the newspapers, some of these groups were the Liberation for Puerto Rico, the Congress of Puerto Rican Hometowns, and the Puerto Rican Socialist Party. Among the jailed leaders were Gilberto Gerena Valentín, a militant leader in the community, and other less wellknown participants. They asked for a "stop to the farce" and claimed there were not Puerto Ricans speaking for the Puerto Rican community, only government officials, and others who did not represent the community.[5]

The dissident elements halted the continuation of the hearings, organized themselves into a group, got money from private donations, and invited Puerto Ricans and other group representatives to bring their grievances to a commission, which, in their opinion, truly represented the interest of the community.

Starting on May 15th, 1972, for a whole week this commission heard testimony at The Brotherhood-in-Action building, transmitted over the radio the full proceedings, and got wide newspaper coverage. The report of the hearings was to be sent to the United States Federal Civil Rights Commission in Washington.[6]

PICKETS AT THE "DAILY NEWS" AND "NEW YORK" MAGAZINE

Some Puerto Rican community leaders had accused the *Daily News* of New York of a consistent discriminatory editorial policy towards Puerto Ricans. In August, 1972, after a series of articles resented by community leaders, the National Puerto Rican Association for Civil Rights leadership and other members of the community met with the editors of the paper. Unsatisfied with the outcome of the meeting, they organized a boycott. The President of the organization was jailed.[7]

The *New York* magazine was also the target of a picket line protesting an article which was "discriminating and derogatory of the Puerto Rican culture." This protest was organized by the League of Puerto Rican Artists and Writers of New York.[8]

Puerto Ricans have radicalized themselves in pressing for other issues such as housing, health services, and education. These issues are of a reformist character and usually attract the support of those leaders in the community who place the advancement and adjustment of the Puerto Ricans in the life of the city as central to their goals. These leaders and their followers seek solutions by reforming the system and seek political power through the polls. Their interest is primarily in New York City, and they do not participate in the affairs of the militant and radical elements who advocate independence for Puerto Rico. They involve themselves in cultural activities with other Spanish speaking groups, and if they have feelings for the solution of the status of the Island do not show them in public demonstrations.

There is another direction in which the militants moved during the sixties. This one was directly connected to the status of the Island, and to what they consider the plight of those oppressed by the present capitalist system. When the civil rights movement developed and gathered strength among the Blacks, and Malcom X became the martyr and symbol of the separatist movement, Puerto Rican radicals looked for his Puerto Rican counterpart and selected Pedro Albizu Campos as their martyr and their symbolism of the cause of independence. Albizu, educated at Harvard, who went to prison and lived in exile in New York for several years, is the subject of a new resurgence of identity among second generation Puerto Ricans. His biography and his portrait, and his writings are widely known by Puerto Ricans who may not know Spanish and perhaps have never even visited the Island.

Fragments from his speeches are used on posters in most of the clubs and organizations of the youth movement and of the militant and radical groups. Together with Che Guevara he is the idol of these groups.

Another name widely used by many Puerto Ricans as a symbol of the struggle is the name of Vito Marcantonio. The independence movement considers him the one voice who brought the plight of the Puerto Ricans to the halls of the Congress of the United States. It is of little importance to these groups that this man was of Italian descent. To them he was a champion of their cause.

New groups responding to a radical and separatist ideology emerged during the sixties. The most famous of all of them was the Young Lords Party.

THE YOUNG LORDS PARTY

The Young Lords were the Puerto Rican counterpart of the Black Panthers, who originated in Chicago and formed an organization in New York City in the summer of 1969. They organized themselves in the styles of a revolutionary party, with a Socialist ideology for the liberation of all the oppressed peoples within the capitalist system. Their national headquarters were located in the heart of Spanish Harlem, near 112th Street and Madison Avenue, with branches in The Bronx, the Lower East Side, Newark, and Philadelphia. The chairman of the party was Felipe Luciano; Juan González, Minister of Education; and Pablo (Yoruba) Guzmán, Minister of Information, were the core of their leadership.

Women constituted about 40 percent of the Young Lords membership. There were two women on the six-member governing Central Committee: Denise Oliver, Minister of Finance; and Gloria Cruz, a field marshal.

Liberation for the women in the party did not come easily. In an interview for *The New York Times* on November 11, 1970, Denise Oliver, 23, said: "When the Young Lords started a year and a half ago, there were very few sisters. We had a hard time being heard at meetings, and most of the work we did was secretarial work." The "machismo" concept caused much in-fighting within the Young Lords, the constant need for the males to assert their masculinity; finally, the group added a plank calling for the equality of women to their revolutionary platform.

The membership roll of the Lords was never revealed; at rallies they rarely exceeded two hundred, with ages ranging from 13 to 28. As an emblem, they wore a purple beret, and for propaganda they published a weekly newspaper, "Pa'lante" (Puerto Rican slang for "right-on").[9]

In December, 1969, they staged a sit-in at Metropolitan Hospital, demanding a halt to the four million two hundred thousand dollars spent on a construction program, until the community was consulted. At that point the group announced that they planned similar demonstrations in "all the hospitals that serve oppressed poeple."[10] They also seized the building of Lincoln Hospital in The Bronx and in July, 1970, they were joined in their protest by members of the "Think Lincoln Committee", a patient-worker committee of the hospital, and by members of the Health Revolutionary Unity Movement, a city-wide committee of hospital workers.[11]

In October, 1970, the Young Lords took up arms, and voicing anger over the death of one of their members in the Tombs, seized the First Spanish Methodist Church. They seized Julio Roldan's coffin from a funeral parlor, occupied the church, and proclaiming the end of their "no weapons" policy, stood guard in the church with guns.[12]

The Young Lords proved to be masters of radical tactics and according to most observers increased the sensitivity of the ghetto institutions to their community. In general, the Puerto Rican community had an ambivalent attitude toward the group; many elements in the community supported them and interceded with the authorities as mediators when there were legal problems. They attracted national attention with their garbage-burning techniques and their political style and rhetoric, winning support for their cause from liberal elements.

The target of the Young Lords in 1970 was the *Desfile Puertorriqueño*, which has been considered a symbol of the day when the unity of the community is demonstrated to all. The Lords were reacting to the polarization in Puerto Rico caused by the victory of the Statehood Party (*Partido Nuevo Progresista*) and the invitation extended to Governor Ferré to be the guest of honor at the Parade. The Lords interrupted the *Desfile* by marching with members of other pro-independence and leftist groups, and by chanting anti-imperialist slogans. Some members of the crowd pelted the Governor with eggs, and the police charged the Lords, arresting some of them.

In my interviews with some of the members of the founders of the *Desfile* I found the reaction mixed. "The polarization in Puerto Rico has oriented the youth to stop using the *Desfile* to glorify the colonial regime. It is being used by the politicians, both here and in Puerto Rico. This *Desfile* will probably disappear if the revolutionary elements grow," said Angel M. Arroyo, a member of the Founders Committee of the PuertoRican Parade. He added that he saw the Lords as a reaction to the socio-economic situation and to discrimination against Puerto Ricans.[13]

A leftist leader, Gilberto Gerena Valentín, who once was the Chairman of the *Desfile*, and is the present leader of the Congress of Hometown Groups, evaluated the militant interference of the Lords as "the imminent radicalization of the *Desfile*, which so far has been the special day for showing pride in being a Puerto Rican. The Lords dramatized the need for a change in the orientation of the *Desfile* and other activities in the community."[14]

The Lords during 1970 and 1971 interrupted or took over practically all of the conferences and activities in which the city government, representatives from Puerto Rico, and the reformist elements of the PuertoRican community participated. These "occupations" were peaceful and were followed by speeches in which the Young Lords explained their program, and their goals for the community. In these efforts they were successful in enlisting the radical youth of the colleges, who were also active in using confrontation tactics to obtain programs of ethnic studies in city and private universities.

In 1972, the Young Lords changed their name to the Organization of Puerto Rican Revolutionary Workers, and even though they subscribe to a revolutionary socialist ideology, their tactics have changed to a continuation of workers' education, to the protection of the democratic rights of the workers, and to the solidarity of the working classes to continue the struggle for these rights.[15]

Even though the Lords advocated independence for PuertoRico, they did not establish formal ties with the Nationalist, or Independence, parties or with the Armed Revolutionary Independentist Movement, MIRA, which claims the credit for terrorist bombings and other terrorist tactics to highlight the colonial status of Puerto Rico.[16] The Lords visited Puerto Rico frequently, and established themselves for a short time in one of the worst slums of San Juan, but eventually withdrew with the conviction that their revolutionary struggle had to be waged among the poor masses residing in the United States.

UNITED FRONT PRO PUERTO RICAN POLITICAL PRISONERS

This movement is composed of different committees both in Puerto Rico and in the United States to raise funds to defend Puerto Ricans who are in jail either in Puerto Rico or in the United States because of some act advocating the independence of Puerto Rico. These groups also collect funds to help politically motivated draft resisters.

There had been political prisoners since the revolt of the Nationalists in Puerto Rico in 1950, since the attacts on Blair House and the House of Representatives in 1954, and from sporadic violent incidents, such as the alleged killing of a policeman by Humberto Pagán, a student from the University of Puerto Rico, and the alleged setting of bombs by Carlos Feliciano in New York.

Since 1968, when the Statehood Party won, the revolutionary acts, especially the setting of fires and the bombing of American factories in Puerto Rico, increased because of the political polarization. The government of Puerto Rico accuses Cuba's Fidel Castro as being partly responsible for these acts.

In New York City the committees to aid political prisoners hold fund raising activities, and concentrate on this issue to bring cohesion to the task of preserving the goal of independence for Puerto Rico as a pressing one, when the migrants face so many problems of coping with living in and adapting themselves to New York City. Many of the members of the committees are young and in colleges, but many others are either *Independentistas* or sympathizers of independence for Puerto Rico. They see this movement as part of their revolutionary struggle for liberation on all fronts: political, social, and economic.

In the *Desfile* celebrated on June 2, 1973, the largest contingent to march in orderly fashion and with a permit from the organizers of the *Desfile* were the different political prisoners' committees, not only from New York City, but from other cities as well, since this is a national movement. They bitterly oppose Congressman Herman Badillo in his political aspirations in New York City, even though he is on record for petitioning clemency for those in jail in letters sent to President Nixon, since 1971.[17]

These groups, in agreement with some of the black radicals, feel that United States prison and judicial systems are prejudiced against the minority group in New York City — Blacks and Puerto Ricans — and that many of those sentenced are political prisoners as well as civil prisoners.

This movement developed a broader appeal and base, gathering impetus after the disastrous riots of most of the nation's prisons.

Other issues that gained support from the radical independents and some liberals during the sixties and up to now have been the practice-bombing of Culebra by the United States Navy, and the inclusion of Puerto Rico by the Committee of Decolonization of the United Nations. Even though the initiation and leadership originated in Puerto Rico, these issues became central to the militant groups who reside in New York City. They attracted the attention of both the Spanish and English press, and as usual, kindled bitter opposition from the conservative elements in the community, who consider these involvements detrimental to the overall advancement and accomodation of the Puerto Rican migrants in New York City.

Simultaneously with the development of these new styles of political action by the militant and radical elements of the community, new forms of political participation also developed: the politics of the Poverty Programs and registration drives to increase the power of the Puerto Ricans at the polls.

FOOTNOTES

1. Nathan Glazer, Daniel Moynihan, *Beyond the Melting Pot* (The MIT Press, Cambridge, Mass. 1963), p.99.
2. John Warren Gotsh, *Puerto Rican Leadership in New York* (Unpublished Master Thesis, Sociology Department, New York University, 1966) Chapter III. *The Anti-Poverty Programs*. Joseph Fitzpatrick. *The Puerto Rican Americans; The Meaning of Migration to the Mainland,* (Prentice Hall, Englewood Cliffs, New Jersey, 1971), p.67.
3. Proceedings of the Mayor's Puerto Rican Community Conference. Mimeograph copies, *Community Development Agency of the City's Human Resources Administration*, 1967.
4. Joseph Fitzpatrick — *The Puerto Rican Americans — The Meaning of Migration to the Mainland*, op. cit., p.69.
5. *The New York Times,* February 15, 1972. *El Diario,* February 16, 1972.
6. *El Diario*, May 15, 16, 17, 18 and 19th, 1972. Coverage of daily developments of the hearings.
   Taped interview with the organizer of the hearings, Gilberto Gerena — Valentín, chairman of the coalition of thirty-five organizations sponsoring the hearings.
7. *El Diario*, August 8, 1972.
8. *El Diario,* August 22, 1972.
9. *Personal interview* with a member of the Young Lords. October 16, 1972.
10. *The New York Times,* Dec. 6, 1969.
11. *The New York Times*, July 15, 1970.
12. *The New York Times*, Oct. 15, 1970.
13. *Taped interview* with Angel M. Arroyo, member of the Founders Committee of the Puerto Rican Parade, July 16, 1972.
14. *Taped interview* with Gilberto Gerena Valentín, President, Congress of Puerto Rican Hometown Groups. July 18, 1972.
15. *El Diario, Marginalia Column* by Luisa Quintero, Aug. 25, 1972.
16. *The New York Times*, July 15, 1970.
17. *El Diario,* December 12, 1972.

CHAPTER VI

POVERTY PROGRAMS AND REGISTRATION DRIVES AS NEW FORMS OF POLITICAL PARTICIPATION

POPULATION

The Census Bureau reported a count of 811,843 persons of Puerto Rican birth or parentage in 1970, a gain of 200,000 over 1960. The Bureau considers them as if they were another traditional European nationality. As older generations pass on and an increasingly larger percentage of Puerto Ricans are born here, the numbers living in the city may actually decline, just as first and second generation Italians, Germans and Irish are much lower in number in New York City than they were a decade ago.

The heaviest concentrations of Puerto Rican residents are as follows:

Manhattan — Lower East Side, Harlem, scattered West Side areas, Washington Heights and Inwood;

The Bronx — Port Morris, Mott Haven, Melrose, Morrisania, Hunts Point, Clason Point and Tremont;

Brooklyn — Williamsburg, East New York, South Brooklyn, Red Hook Sunset Park, parts of Fort Greene and the edge of Bedford Stuyvesant;

Queens — Corona, Corona East and Elmhurst.

The official breakdown of the Puerto Rican population by boroughs was as follows:[1]

	1960	1970	Percent Population of Total (1970)
The Bronx	186,885	316,772	21.5
Brooklyn	180,114	271,769	10.4
Manhattan	225,639	185,323	12.
Queens	17,432	33,141	1.7
Staten Island	2,504	4,838	1.6
City — Total	612,574	811,843	10.3

The Puerto Rican community leaders contended that there was a drastic undercount of Puerto Ricans in the 1970 census. They said that the low count severely injures their political power and their chances for obtaining sufficient Federal economic aid, such as antipoverty money. Their own estimates had ranged from one million to 1,300,000. Even the Department of Labor of the State had put the actual figure at 1,050,000. The Migration Division of the Commonwealth of Puerto Rico estimated the figure at 1,300,000.

The community leaders also contended that the Census Bureau's total was a projection based on a 15% sample of areas where Puerto Ricans were thought to live. The Bureau counts as Puerto Ricans only those residents who were born in Puerto Rico or who had at least one parent born there — the first two generations. Third generation Puerto Ricans, who are growing in number, are not counted as Puerto Ricans.[2]

An *ad hoc* group called the Puerto Rican Hispanic Populace Coalition Committee asked that all Puerto Ricans be counted, including the third generation. They noted that a black is counted as a black regardless of his generation. In fact they charged that some Puerto Ricans are counted as blacks rather than Puerto Ricans. The census figures show that blacks in the city in 1970 outnumbered Puerto Ricans by a little better than 2 to 1 — a total of 1,665,000 to 812,000.[3]

Regarding color classification, the census classified Puerto Ricans as Puerto Rican — whites and Puerto Ricans — blacks. The other categories were whites (not including Puerto Ricans), blacks, and "others." The Census Bureau calculated conservatively that 90 percent of the Puerto Ricans listed themselves as white. The Bureau of the Community Council of Greater New York estimated the black, the Puerto Rican, and "other races" of New York City at 35 percent of the total population and expanding rapidly.[4] The Council's estimates also reported one million black and Puerto Rican residents added to the city's population during the sixties.

SEGREGATION AND POVERTY AREAS

A detailed analysis by *The New York Times* of official census figures found two-thirds of the city's 2,159 census tracts to be either 90 percent white or 90 percent black. The population of whites (exclusive of Puerto Ricans) dropped by one million between 1960 and 1970. Where census tracts had a mixed population it was very frequently a case of a minority expanding rapidly into old white areas.

The Research Division of the Human Resources Administration estimates that 816 percent of the black population in 1970 lived in the 26 officially designated poverty areas. During the decade, the black population in those poverty ares grew by more than 380,000 — from 980,000 to 1,361,000. The Research Division estimated an overall Puerto Rican gain in those areas of about 400,000.

The Bureau of Labor Statistics in a year-long study found that more than half of the 85,700 Puerto Ricans who live in poverty areas make up the poorest bloc of people in the city. According to the study they have the most trouble getting and keeping jobs if they are well, and many have physical or mental disabilities that make it useless for them to go looking for a job. Others work for less than minimum wages or can get only part-time jobs. Puerto Ricans are the least skilled and the least educated. In this particular study unemployment averaged 4 percent among the men who headed households.

In the core poverty areas — Central and East Harlem, The South Bronx and Bedford-Stuyvesant in Brooklyn — among 26,100 Puerto Ricans headed households, there were nearly twice as many unemployed as there were white men heads of households.[5]

The 1970 census found that persons of Spanish speaking ancestry earned significantly greater incomes than blacks, even though they had poorer education. The typical family income in 1970 was $7,330 for families of Spanish origin, $6,280 for blacks, and $10,240 for whites. Puerto Rican families, however, earned less than the families of Spanish-origin or the blacks.[6]

Because of this situation of poverty, unemployment, and underemployment, Puerto Ricans depend in large numbers on public welfare for their subsistence. Puerto Ricans constitute approximately 39 percent of the poverty families, and they constitute about 40 percent of persons on welfare.[7] The issue is a complicated one, since it involves both the problem of public welfare throughout the nation and the problem of possible weakening and disorganization of the Puerto Rican family because of migration. The extent to which public welfare helps the family in this process of adaptation to the city, or accelerates the dislocation of the family as a unit, is a dilemma for social workers and researchers to further explore. Welfare recipients have contributed in no small proportion to the stigmatization of Puerto Ricans in New York City, and they meet with social disapproval from both the receiving community and the migrant community.

POVERTY PROGRAMS

The anti-poverty programs for the Puerto Rican community represented the opportunity to further develop the organization of the community. Here was, at last, the opportunity to finance the programs the groups and organizations had long envisaged but were unable to implement because of the poverty of the migrants. Some of this implementation has been accomplished, but the path has been far from easy, and, as stated before, involved the Puerto Rican leadership in conflict with the black minority group which shared the poverty and the ills of ghetto living with the migrants. At the end of the sixties these two minorities found themselves the target of the frustrations of other ethnic groups who also claimed that they had been overlooked by the anti-poverty programs and by other city, state and federal programs designed to elevate the social and economic status of the disadvantaged in the city.

From the very beginning of the anti-poverty program, the struggle for the control of programs and agencies have been waged on two fronts — the Council Against Poverty and the 26 community corporations, umbrella agencies for anti-poverty programs. The corporations decide which anti-poverty programs should be established in its area and allocate city, state or federal funds for the programs.

Puerto Ricans won control of the major anti-poverty umbrella groups of The Bronx: Hunts Point, the South Bronx, and Tremont. They have also won considerable influence in Williamsburg, Coney Island and Sunset Park in

Brooklyn, and the Lower East Side, Lower West Side and West Side of Manhattan.

The pattern of gaining control of a corporation is, first, to get the vote out to elect Puerto Ricans to the board of governors. Usually control by Puerto Ricans of governing boards is followed by a decision of the Council Against Poverty, ordering the board to give blacks an ethnic balance. Puerto Ricans generally protested, contending that when blacks were in control Puerto Ricans did not get ethnic balance.[8]

Puerto Ricans, for example, have denounced the Council Against Poverty as black-dominated.

The 51-member Council is appointed by the Mayor; it has a majority of blacks, and only eight Puerto Ricans. The city claims they have followed Federal guidelines. Rifts and leadership confrontation between Puerto Ricans and blacks have marked the relationship and work of the members of the Council. A rift developed to such a point that Mayor John Lindsay had to appoint a mediating panel to write out recommendations for the Council's functioning. However, with the impending cuts in federal funds for this, and other programs, all groups are closing ranks behind the Mayor to demand funds for the city.

To the charges of Puerto Rican leaders of favoritism towards the blacks the city answered with a report that about 22 percent of the $175.4 million spent in 1971 was assigned to Puerto Rican projects. The report also claimed that although Puerto Ricans are the major group in only three of twenty-six poverty areas, ten of the areas' community corporations have a majority of Puerto Rican members on their boards of directors, or a Puerto Rican as their executive director, or both. Two hundred Puerto Rican organizations were reported to be financed through the Community Development Agency, the city agency supervising the work of the community corporations.[9]

FROM CLUBHOUSES TO ANTI-POVERTY PROGRAMS

From the very beginning, the Puerto Rican community leaders saw the poverty programs as a tool for increasing their political power in the city. The struggle to control the community corporations, even though it had the negative effect of stirring animosity with black groups, was seen as inevitable to the control of a share of the thousands of jobs and millions of dollars of the anti-poverty programs. The community leaders saw the agencies as training grounds for political leadership for Puerto Ricans, very much as earlier waves of immigrants used clubhouses as training sources.

The participations in elections for boards of community corporations are experiences which lead to a more actively involved community, where the power of the individual's vote is translated into control of a community agency. Larger numbers of Puerto Ricans also learned to speak up in neighborhood and city-wide meetings, and to organize for representation of community needs. Since the community corporations control jobs, this is a strong incentive for participation. It anticipates what an increase of voting power could mean for the advancement of the group city-wide. The young feel more attracted by these anti-poverty programs than by the clubhouses' political activities, which are largely dominated by the older and long-established political groups in the community.

Three Puerto Rican agencies which had been established during the mid-1950's with private funds and donations benefited from funds from the anti-poverty programs. These were the Puerto Rican Forum, dedicated to the development of Puerto Rican leadership in business, education and civic affairs; Aspira, founded in 1961, dedicated to provide guidance to Puerto Rican youth for continuing their education and to entering college; and the Puerto Rican Family Institute, which has a social work approach to the problems faced by the families who migrate.

In the field of community action, two projects are the outstanding result of anti-poverty programs, The Puerto Rican Community Development Project and the Multi-Service Center of Hunts Point in The Bronx. The goal of the Puerto Rican Community Development Project is to develop a strong, stable immigrant community which will eventually enable migrants to move into the main stream of American society. It was first founded in 1965. It has developed programs in job training, tutoring programs, neighborhood youth corps, addiction prevention programs, and a block program of community organization. It has developed over the years as a civic and social representative agency of the Puerto Rican community.

The block program is the backbone of the community participation program of the Project. One hundred Puerto Rican groups entered into contract arrangements with the Project, receiving financial assistance and training from the Project's central staff. Most of these groups had been already organized in the late 40's, 50's, and early 60's. They were ready for the assistance and resources which the project was able to provide. They flourish under this arrangement, and when they have successfully worked themselves into self-sustaining organizations, they stop their contract with the Project, allowing another group in need of services to benefit from it. These leaders have brought new layers of leadership into activities and programs, creating a militant and forceful group representing the neighborhoods where Puerto Ricans reside. They are now easily mobilized, and their participation has enabled the Puerto Rican community to take great strides in social civic and political affairs.

Their role is paramount in the organizing of the main cultural activities of the community, such as the annual Puerto Rican *Desfile* (Parade), the *Fiesta Folklórica* (Puerto Rican Folklore Festival), celebrated every year for a whole day in Central Park, and the Catholic *Fiesta de San Juan* which is civic and cultural even though sponsored by the New York Archdiocese.

The central staff, including the director, assistant director, and the sixty members of the board of the Project, quickly project themselves into leadership positions in the city on behalf of the Puerto Ricans. This particular

Project constitutes a training ground for leaders, who make the contacts and resources and assume representation for the groups and community.

The Multi-Service Center of Hunts Point in The Bronx has a similar program, with a primary goal of health and health services. Its director, Ramón S. Vélez, is one of the outstanding political leaders in the Puerto Rican community. Commanding a great deal of patronage through jobs in his programs, Vélez has consolidated gains in the South Bronx and has been called an "anti-poverty czar." He works in close collaboration with the leaders of the Puerto Rican Community Development Project and in political association with Congressman Herman Badillo, the foremost political leader of the Puerto Ricans in the city's Democratic Party.

These programs developed during the sixties, have enabled Puerto Ricans to organize themselves internally to be able to participate in the life of the city to an extent that they had never been able to do before. There is a great deal of factionalism and strife within these structures, but the struggles the leaders had to engage in during the formative years of the agencies and programs have helped to develop a pattern of cooperation which may result in increasing power in the civic and political arena of the life of the city. The recent drive to register Puerto Ricans to vote is an example of how these leaders united with other leaders of the overall Puerto Rican community to launch a campaign to increase the numbers of Puerto Ricans eligible to vote. The development of this campaign since its beginnings in the early fifties is an illustration of the development and patterns of participation of the Puerto Rican leaders and their groups.

LA CRUZADA CIVICA DEL VOTO
(The Voting Civic Crusade)

The above was the title given by Puerto Ricans to their drive to register more Puerto Ricans to make them eligible voters. This was a non-partisan drive. The committee was formed with representatives of all the New York City political parties. It was begun shortly after the Democratic National Convention of Miami in 1972, and was stimulated by Senator George MacGovern's plan to register the minorities, including youth and women, to increase his constituency.

The first Puerto Rican community campaigns for registration were launched in the early fifties, when the Puerto Rican migration was yearly swelling up to 50,000. The target number during those days show the great struggle the leaders had to overcome in getting the migrants to register and vote. The central point for organization, direction, printing and distribution of informational materials was the Migration Division of the Commonwealth of Puerto Rico. Campaigns were organized on a non-partisan basis. Since the majority of Puerto Ricans vote Democratic, there was usually a larger representation of this party. The Division was also an arm of the government of Puerto Rico, and the Popular Democratic Party was in close cooperation and affiliation (informal) with the National Democratic Party and the city's democratic administration.

The Puerto Rican community groups sent their representatives and members to give voluntary services, as did the political clubs and organizations. Loudspeakers were sent to the different areas of population concentration to deliver information in Spanish. Radio spot announcements were recorded with the voice of outstanding leaders urging Puerto Ricans to register and vote. The first brochure had a target of 35,000 registrants as a goal. When the Division counted it, it fell short of the target.

The motto of the 1972 *Cruzada Cívica del Voto* when it started in February was "100,000 new voters."[11] The first organization to start the drive was the daily newspaper, *El Diario de Nueva York*. Members of the Puerto Rican organizations, especially the Puerto Rican Development Project, came in large numbers to inaugurate the campaign.

The Spanish Chapter of the State League of Women Voters also took the drive as their number one project, participating as volunteers and sponsoring conferences to meet those Puerto Ricans who were to run in the June 1972 primaries.[12] The increasing number of Puerto Rican candidates for the primaries added new interest to the registration campaign. The fact that Herman Badillo was running for re-election in his Bronx Congressional District 21 was another incentive for many Puerto Ricans to re-elect their first Congressman. Every possible opportunity was used by the organizers, from going to the Yankee Stadium and setting up tables at the entrance to marathons over the radio and T.V., to collect funds and calls from promising registrants.

The Puerto Rican Development Project assumed the leadership and centralization of the services. The Migration Division cooperated, but the leadership had shifted to the anti-poverty organizations and its leaders. The President of the Cruzada was Ramón Vélez, the Executive Director of the Multi-Service Center of The Bronx.

By August of 1972, according to the Cruzada, they had already met their goal of 100,000 and raised it to "150,000 new voters." In a press conference at the City's Board of Election, the leaders delivered their registration records to the Board's Commissioners.[13]

The regular registration period is in October. The Cruzada joined this effort and announced that they were aiming at "200,000 new voters."[14]

City-wide this effort lagged; however, the Board acknowledged that for the first time the numbers added to the city registered voters were higher than the previous election period. One reason was the registration of the eighteen-year-olds; no doubt the Puerto Rican effort was adding to the usual numbers of prior years.[15]

In a personal interview I had with James Siket, Executive Director of the New York City Board of Elections, when I was trying to find out the results of the Cruzada, he outlined the policy of the Board as: "Not giving any official estimates of ethnic breakdowns. They keep no records by age or nationality, only by party affiliation and sex."[16]

Political analysts of previous drives speculated that even though the Puerto Rican community had substantially increased its voting potential, many factors contributed to the lagging at the polls compared to those registered. There is always a high mobility of Puerto Ricans within the city. With a change of address comes a new neighborhood, and the need to re-establish communication with candidates and political leaders. It may take time before political participation and involvement is resumed.

Many errors are committed in the process of registration which can actually invalidate the registered voter to vote in primaries; por example, not identifying the party to which they belong, or identifying the wrong party. Redistricting in New York City changed the boundaries of many districts and the polling places for the voters, making it difficult for them to find the right polling place on election day.

In spite of this and many others factors, there is no doubt that the leadership exercised by these groups gave impetus to the political participation of Puerto Ricans. The November 1972 elections and the Mayoralty primaries might show such results.

In their quest for political power the migrants have been able to increase their resources and develop programs with new forms of political participation.

In the next chapter, we shall see however, in considering the mayoralty primary runoff, to what extent, in spite of these new resources, the leaders still depend on support from the Island.

FOOTNOTES

1. *The New York Times*, October 2, 1972.
2. *El Diario de Nueva York*, February 2, 1972.
3. *The New York Times*, October 2, 1972.
4. *The New York Times*, March 6, 1972.
5. *The New York Times*, November 17, 1969.
6. The Bureau of the Census, Current Population Reports, *Family Income of Spanish Speaking Families in the United States,* (No. 224, Superintendent of Documents, Washington, 1971), p.20.
7. Joseph P. Fitzpatrick, *Puerto Rican Americans* (Prentice-Hall, Inc., Englewood Cliffs, New Jersey, 1971), p.158.
8. *Personal interview with Mr. Federico Perez,* Assistant Director of the Puerto Rican Community Development Project. October 17, 1972.
9. The *New York Times,* March 22, 1971.
10. *Puerto Rican Community Development Project,* Summary of Programs operated by the Puerto Rican Community Development Project, 1972.
11. *The New York Times,* August 16, 1969.
12. *El Diario de Nueva York,* February 9, 1972, and *Cruzada Cívica del Voto*, informational material.
13. *El Diario de Nueva York*, August 5, 1972.
14. *El Diario de Nueva York*, August 26, 1972.
15. *The New York Times*, September 9, 1972.
16. *Personal interview with James Siket*, Executive Director, New York City Board of Elections.

CHAPTER VII

THE PUERTO RICANS AND PARTY POLITICS: INTERLINKS BETWEEN NEW YORK CITY AND THE ISLAND

THE DEMOCRATS

The political activity of Puerto Ricans in New York City continues to be predominantly participation in the politics of the Democratic Party. This party loyalty has been assailed by some observers as the reason for their lack of representation in the political arena; others feel that it is only within this party that the political future of the migrants may eventually be of importance and value to both the party and the community.

Back in 1969, the prospects were bleak. Making up no more than 10 percent of the city's population, Puerto Ricans were facing the prospect of finding themselves with no political representation in the city. Herman Badillo, Borough President of The Bronx, in order to run in the Democratic mayoralty primary had not sought re-election. He made a good showing, but lost. The two Puerto Rican City Councilmen would not continue to hold office after January, 1970. The Puerto Rican representation in Albany consisted of a State Senator, who ran unopposed and was backed by the three parties, and three Puerto Rican assemblymen from The Bronx, Manuel Ramos, Armando Montano and Luis Nine.

Analysts and observers of the community give various reasons for this situation: no concentrated power in particular districts due to dispersion and State re-districting; opposition to Puerto Ricans by other Puerto Rican candidates in the areas where there is a high concentration of Puerto Ricans, as in the case of the two lost councilmanic districts of the South Bronx and East Harlem. Others consider that most second generation Puerto Ricans are too young to vote. The remoteness of the candidates and the uncertainty about the issues was another factor frequently mentioned. Many Puerto Ricans also were showing a great deal of disillusionment with party politics in the city, particularly with their failure to achieve participation in the regular Democratic club houses, and with their patronizing attitudes of the reform Democrats and the white Liberals' attitude toward the migrants.

In the 1969 campaign, only five of the 246 candidates running for office were Puerto Ricans. All of them lost.[1]

Glazer and Moynihan, in their introduction to the second edition of *Beyond the Melting Pot*, wrote in 1970:

> Of the Catholic groups in the city, none ended the 1960's in less promising circumstances than did the Puerto Ricans. The expectation voiced in *Beyond the Melting Pot* that they would leapfrog their black neighbors does not seem to have occurred. To the contrary, Puerto Ricans emerged from the decade as the group with the highest incidence of poverty and the

lowest number of men in public position who bargain and broker the arrangements of the city.[2]

Writing in 1971, Father Joseph Fitzpatrick, dealing with the question of political representation also sounded a pessimistic note as the political prospects of Puerto Ricans. Except for the rise of Herman Badillo as the outstanding political figure of the Puerto Rican community, and his impressive rise to power, Fitzpatrick joined the ranks of those who were looking for the reasons for this dismal prospect. In agreement with other observers, he acknowledged the loyalty of Puerto Ricans to the Democratic Party. "Hubert Humphrey received about 93 percent of the Puerto Rican vote in 1968 . . . . The vote in predominantly Puerto Rican East Harlem was 88 percent for Hulan Jack, a black candidate for the State Assembly on the Democratic ticket, against 12 percent for a Puerto Rican on the Republican ticket."[3]

The 1972 campaign for the Democratic National ticket marked an increase in the participation of Puerto Ricans within the party. The first in the series of events was the early endorsement of Senator George McGovern by Herman Badillo and by most of the Puerto Rican democratic leaders. McGovern visited the Bronx in early February and came to East Harlem, participated in rallies, and stimulated and endorsed candidates for delegates to the Miami convention. In the June 20th primaries Puerto Ricans elected eleven delegates to the Convention.

The total Puerto Rican delegation from New York City was eighteen — eleven elected, five at-large, and two alternates. From the very beginning, the strategy of the Puerto Ricans at the Convention was to join with the Chicano and other Spanish speaking delegates from other states to form a *Latino Caucus*. This they did, with one hundred and sixty-one elected delegates, and seventy-two alternates. The Chicanos were the largest single Spanish bloc. Puerto Rican delegates from Puerto Rico also joined. This *Caucus* bargained within the Convention for issues and positions favorable to their constituencies, such as bilingual education as an objective in education. This *Latino Caucus* was twice as large as the 1968 one, giving some hope nationally to the group.[4]

Puerto Ricans felt frustrated at the Convention, but one particular aspect was important: they came back to New York with plans drawn for the registration drive they launched in the following months. This leadership found solidarity with other Spanish speaking groups, who considered the Puerto Rican vote in the Northwest as strategically important in their political plans. The drive by Senator McGovern to register minorities and the drive to enlist the support of youth encouraged this group of leaders in their plans.[5]

Herman Badillo was the undisputed leader of the Puerto Ricans and his leadership was re-affirmed by the recognition given him by the Chicanos in electing him as co-chairman with Senator Joseph Bernal of Texas of the *Latino Caucus* within the Democratic Party.

This group of delegates to the Convention continued to meet in New York City and kept the community informed of their plans for registration for the November elections. With the lowering of the voting age to eighteen years the voting potential of the Puerto Rican community is now estimated at close to half a million.

In the Presidential election year more Puerto Rican candidates than ever ran for office — fourteen in all. Even though the results were far from the goal, Badillo was re-elected to Congress, Senator Robert García to the State Senate, and four Assemblymen were elected to the Albany Assembly.

In early 1973, Congressman Herman Badillo announced his intention to enter the mayoralty primary. Once more Badillo with his political drive was to lead the Puerto Rican democrats in a campaign which from its very beginning was marked by the polarization and the ethnic and racial strife which is dividing the city.

THE DEMOCRATIC LEADER — HERMAN BADILLO

Herman Badillo, who is 43 years old, went into city government in January of 1962, when Mayor Wagner appointed him a deputy real estate commissioner. Within eleven months he was named the city's first relocation commissioner; at the age of 32 he was the youngest full commissioner in the city's history.

These first steps in politics were remarkable achievements for an orphan whose parents had died of tuberculosis in Puerto Rico when he was five years old. He came to New York when he was eleven, worked his way as dishwasher, pin boy, and cook; he attended Harlem High School, City College (graduated *magna cum laude*) and Brooklyn Law School (valedictorian).

He was married to two different Jewish women. His present wife, Irma Leibling, is an active campaigner for her husband. Besides climbing in politics, the Badillos have achieved middle class status, having started in a flat in East Harlem, where he formed his own reform club, the John F. Kennedy Democratic Club. He was elected Borough President of The Bronx in 1965. He resigned in the spring of 1969 to run in the mayoralty primary but was defeated. He ran for Congress in 1970 in a tri-borough district covering portions of the South Bronx, upper Manhattan and Queens. He was re-elected to the 21st Congressional District in The Bronx in 1972.[6]

As described by Richard Reeves, journalist, "Badillo is not a humble man, he is not a soft man, and the word 'cool' has been and has to be overused in describing him." Described as a "man behind a mask" he has been known to say," I never begged. I would rather starve."[7]

Badillo's political style in his 1969 mayoralty primary was described by many as that of a liberal reformist catering to the middle classes of the city, and was a far cry from the style Puerto Ricans generally look for in their political representatives. It was generally acknowledged during those days that Badillo had "learned the political game," but that his prime objective was not to be the classic ethnic politician. His backers and supporters were predominantly Jewish, but included upperclass Protestants. His career seemed to be cut to fit a direction that would take him away from his ethnicity and into the mainstream of political life of the already changing city.[8]

The positions Badillo took were consistently liberal. He opposed the Vietnam War when it was not then fashionable for a politician to do so openly, and steadily carved for himself a leadership position in New York City's Reform Movement, even though his style had always been coalition politics of regulars and reformers.

In the 1973 mayoralty primary Badillo was expected to win the endorsement of the New Democratic Coalition which was to celebrate its convention on March 3rd. To a certain extent, Badillo himself was somewhat overconfident of getting the endorsement and did not campaign as much in the Reform Clubs as other candidates did. Political experts have analyzed the results of the convention and still are marvelling at the political maneuvering that took place on the floor of that convention, giving the endorsement to the winner, Albert Blumenthal, who was subsequently chosen as mayoral candidate by the Liberal Party, assuring him a place on the ballot in November, 1973.[9]

For a while Badillo was left with few of his backers, except for the full support of the Puerto Rican community in New York and the support of the people of Puerto Rico. Badillo took several trips to Puerto Rico and got the commitment of a committee of political and business leaders to raise funds for his campaign. Most of the money that came into Badillo's headquarters during April and May, before the June 4th primary, came from Puerto Rico.

The mayors of many Puerto Rican towns and cities and other government and business leaders came to New York to campaign in the Puerto Rican neighborhood clubs and organizations.

Instead of being completely discouraged by the NDC nonendorsement, the Badillo campaign picked up a new and different spirit. Puerto Ricans and some reform friends and supporters changed the style of the campaign, and Badillo himself became more of an ethnic candidate responding to the new momentum of his campaign.[10]

During the months prior to the primary no activity in the community was celebrated without an invitation to Badillo, the Puerto Rican candidate. Spanish newspapers daily gave news of the campaigns, as did radio and television. The organizers of the Puerto Rican *Desfile*, which was celebrated two days before the primary, chose Badillo as the Grand Marshall of the *Desfile*, an honor they had consistently denied him so far. The mood of the *Desfile* was one of joy, anticipation, and pride. The Governor of Puerto Rico and the mayors who participated all encouraged Badillo on his bid. This was free publicity for the candidate.[11]

There was opposition to Badillo from the radicals and independentistas, and from the Committees for the Freedom of Political Prisoners. They chanted slogans whose chief targets were Badillo and Ramón S. Vélez, the Esecutive Director of the Multi-Service Center of the Bronx, who for these elements represents the classic colonial mediator. Newspapers and banners circulated, but they could not counteract the tide, which was pro-Badillo.

For the first time in the history of political participation by Puerto Ricans in New York City, Puerto Ricans came out to vote "en masa." The atmosphere of political clubs in Puerto Rican sections in East Harlem, the Bronx, and other areas were very similar to those in the Puerto Rican towns during elections. There could be no doubt that the Puerto Rican in New York had a leader. He had emerged and was pulling them out of their apathy to participate in the political process.[12]

The identification with Badillo cut across class lines. The poor called him "un sufrido como yo." (a suffering one like me). The middle classes found the leader who could articulate issues and positions in a political style akin to their own way of thinking.

Abraham Beame got the largest percentage of the vote, but the real hero of the primary was Badillo, who from the underdog position had risen to second place. With new endorsements and funds, Badillo started his runoff campaign for June 26. Even though the enthusiasm was great in the same ethnic circles, plus reform backing, Badillo was badly defeated by Beame.

Political analysts have given many reasons for Badillo's defeat. The main ones are that the heavy turnout in Brooklyn, Queens, and some areas in The Bronx showed that the regular machine could still pull out the vote, and that more than any other factor this had been an anti-Badillo vote, an anti-minority move by the white majority of the city.

Glazer and Moynihan in their analysis of the city had characterized the mood of the city at the beginning of the seventies as one where ethnicity and race were the predominant factors in politics. The question for them was to what extent ethnicity was covering up for racism.[13]

This is a difficult question to answer, but there is little doubt that the polarization in the city is proceeding at a very fast pace, and that the liberal candidate of the late sixties who could articulate positions and lead these groups had suddenly been considered as a Puerto Rican candidate who had to be stopped "for the good of the city." This theme, which was used by the Beame campaign, had helped to mobilize large numbers to come out to vote on June 26.

The role of Puerto Ricans in the city's political climate is difficult indeed. They form a minority group, but a minority which predominantly had seen itself in an immigrant entity from which it could emerge. It is a racially mixed group, but with the gains of the sixties, the group expected that the same programs which helped the Blacks fight prejudice and discrimination would eventually help the fringe minorities and Puerto Ricans to struggle for their civil rights and equality. However, these programs at present have antagonized other ethnic groups, who consider that there has been too much compensation for the Blacks and Puerto Ricans, and that a more conservative policy should be established to put a stop to this trend.

Politicians are aware of this attitude of the majority of the voters and already some liberals have moved considerably to the center. In the midst of it all, there is one gain for the Puerto Rican group; they saw how close they were to organizing themselves into a political bloc proportionate to their numbers and who, upon entering in political coalitions, could increase their political representation, which at present is very minimal. It is difficult to predict which way Puerto Ricans will vote in the elections in November, 1973. There is no doubt disillusionment with the Democratic Party leaders, both with the reforms and regulars, but if the party loyalty continues, these wounds could be healed as politicians woo the increasing number of Puerto Ricans who register and vote.

THE REPUBLICANS

Puerto Rican Republicans are a minority within a minority. To be a Republican in Puerto Rico means to favor statehood as a solution to the status problems of the Island. Those Republicans who migrate continue holding on to their ideology and become assimilationists for those who reside here and for the Island as well. During the first migration period Republicans were a majority party in Puerto Rico within the Coalition Party, that is, Republicans and Socialists united in power. The Resident Commissioners of Puerto Rico in Washington, Santiago Iglesias Pantín and Bolívar Pagán were members of that coalition, and represented the spoils of the Socialist Party.

In an interview I taped with a Republican who migrated in the late twenties, he described the incident in which Commissioner Iglesias was brought to New York City to address a meeting of Puerto Rican leaders. The *independentistas* picketed the locale where the meeting was taking place and they had to take him out of the place with a police escort.[14] In spite of living in the United States, Republicans seem to have problems in attracting large numbers to their ranks.

The first Puerto Rican assemblyman during the thirties was a Republican, but since then no other elected Puerto Rican politician has been a Republican.

According to Commissioner Ruperto Ruiz, a lifelong Republican, the triumph of the Popular Democratic Party in Puerto Rico during the forties and in the Roosevelt Administrations has made it difficult for the U.S. Republican Party of N.Y. to make inroads into the ranks of the migrants. The role of the Migration Division of the Commonwealth of Puerto Rico as the outstanding representative for the community and organizer of so many activities on behalf of the migrant is also cited as a reason for the lack of Republican success.

The only Republican who has really attracted Puerto Ricans in large numbers to vote for him is Governor Nelson Rockefeller. This attraction is attributed to his style as a politician and the fact that he is an expert in Inter-American affairs and has a good command of Spanish. John V. Lindsay also attracted Puerto Ricans in 1965, but Abe Beame got more Democratic votes from the Puerto Rican community than did Lindsay.

Nixon's last campaign drew a fairly good support from the Puerto Rican community and a great deal of this support can be attributed to the efforts of a group of Republicans who constituted themselves into the "Young Puerto Ricans Republican Club." They campaigned extensively, coordinating some of their activities with the Republican Luis A. Ferré, who was Governor of Puerto Rico from 1968 to 1972. Ferré lent support to this group, and during these years the Office of the Migration Division closely co-operated with the efforts of the Republicans in New York City. This group's leaders are usually representatives of the business and social élite of Puerto Rico, closely associated with the branches of Puerto Rican banks and industries which have business on the Island.[15]

One strong source of support during these years, especially after 1968, has been the fact that many of the Federal and State jobs favored Republicans. The Northeast Regional office of the Office of Economic Opportunity is headed by a staunch Puerto Rican Republican who also favored to a large extent his Republican partisans to fill the policy positions of his Region.

Puerto Ricans went to the Republican Convention in Miami. The delegates' group consisted of six members. They joined the group of delegates from Puerto Rico who were headed by Governor Luis A. Ferré. According to the newspapers this group was even more disgruntled than those delegates who went to the Democratic Convention. They protested to Governor Rockefeller, especially against the way Elliot Richardson dealt with the minorities at the Convention.[16]

The Puerto Rico Republican leaders work closely with the two U.S. Republican senators from New York, Senators Jacob Javits and James Buckley, whose offices usually have Spanish-speaking personnel as a liaison with the Puerto Rican and other Hispanic minorities in the city and state.

The Cubans, on the other hand, are predominantly U.S. Republicans, pro-Nixon and pro-assimilation. Their conservative attitude is a source of strain in the relationships between the refugee Cuban community and the migrants from Puerto Rico.

Trying to get estimates of the number of Puerto Ricans who vote Republican is a frustrating experience. No leader ventures any estimates, but they contend that as the community adjusts and accommodates to life in the United States more Puerto Ricans will turn to the Republican Party, as other immigrants have done when larger proportions of their population reach the middle and lower-middle income brackets.

THE LIBERALS

The New York Liberal Party has also sought the votes of the Puerto Ricans, and in the case of Puerto Rican union members who belong to the International Ladies Garment Union, and other affiliated unions, they have been successful in attracting responsible leaders to their ranks.

In the early 1950s the Liberals organized a Spanish Division headed at the beginning by Mrs. Encarnación Padilla de Armas, well-known in the community. They organized groups, particularly of women who are active campaigners and leaders in most of the community activities.[17]

Many Puerto Ricans who are in a middle class bracket vote for the New York's Liberal Party candidates, and the president of the party, Reverend Donald Harrington, is a familiar figure in many of the activities of the Puerto Rican community.

Liberals dispense their patronage, especially in the Relocation department of the city, and favor some of the loyal supporters of the party. The Democrats, however, have always managed to slow down defection from their ranks and have kept the Puerto Rican vote predominantly in their camp.

The power of Puerto Ricans in New York based on party politics still depends to a large extent on the kind of support received from the Island. Consequently Puerto Rican gubernatorial elections are decisive for the New York Puerto Ricans. On the other hand, increased electoral success on the mainland could influence politics in Puerto Rico. As New York Puerto Ricans become a more powerful political bloc, with more strength as a lobby in Washington, they would try to influence the situation on the Island as American Jews try to influence the situation in Israel because of their force as a lobby in American politics.

As New York's Puerto Ricans acquire more political power the interlinks between Puerto Rico and mainland party politics deepen and become more complex.

To add to this already complex situation New York Puerto Ricans have an increasingly difficult situation in their relationships with other Hispanic groups who reside and interrelate with them in the city. In the next chapter, I shall point out the relationship with the Hispanic groups.

FOOTNOTES

1. *The New York Times,* October 15, 1969.
2. Nathan Glazer and Daniel P. Moynihan, *Beyond the Melting Pot,* (MIT Press, Cambridge, 1970. Second Edition), p.xix.
3. Joseph P. Fitzpatrick *Puerto Rican American,* (Prentice Hall, Inc. Englewood Cliffs, New Jersey, 1971), p.58.
4. *El Diario de Nueva York,* July 29, 1972.
5. Ibid., July 14, 1972.
6. *The New York Times,* April 2, 1973.
7. *New York Magazine,* April 10, 1973.
8. *The New York Times Sunday Magazine,* June 3, 1973 (Article *Running for the Unrunnable,* by Tom Buckley).
9. The Village Voice, March 8, 1973 (Article- *The Browning of NDC, From Here to Tammany* by Phil Tracy).
10. *El Diario de Nueva York,* February 16, 1973.
11. *The New York Times,* June 3, 1973.
12. Participant observation by writer, primary day June 4, 1973, at Yorkville-East Harlem Democratic Club, 2012 Second Avenue. Visits to the electoral colleges of the District 68 Part D. The leader, Mr. Eugene Nardelli, was *interviewed* on the political behavior of Puerto Ricans.
13. Glazer and Moynihan, op. cit., p. xxxviii.
14. *Taped Interview* with *Commissioner Ruperto Ruiz,* State Human Rights Commission. August 8, 1972.
15. *El Diario de Nueva York,* November 27, 1972.
16. Ibid., August 24, 1972.
17. *Taped Interview* with Mrs. Encarnación Padilla de Armas. August 5, 1972.

CHAPTER VIII

PUERTO RICANS, CUBANS AND DOMINICANS: THE POLITICS OF HISPANISMO

Since their arrival Puerto Rican migrants have identified themselves with other Spanish speaking groups. The groups call themselves, and in turn are called by the overall New York City community, "hispanos" or "latinos." In setting themselves apart by a stress on ideals and patterns of behavior different from the dominant Anglo culture, Puerto Ricans find themselves with great cultural similarities to those groups who speak Spanish and have a hispanic culture. A feeling of solidarity is developed, based on elements which are basic to the cultural nationalism of the group.

This solidarity was encountered by C. W. Mills and his associates in their study of the Harlem and Morrisania areas of New York, back in 1948. Mills pointed to a possible growth of Spanish consciousness among Puerto Ricans in New York which could involve "the adoption of lifeways and social values somewhat different from those prevalent in Puerto Rico but different also from those of the generalized (middle class) American." He then pointed to the emergence of this consciousness from folkways to formal organizations.[1]

There is strong evidence to suggest that this feeling of identity rests first of all in a common language and in a community feeling maintained by the Spanish tradition in the new world, which cuts across nationality; which makes these groups reject things American.

As Mills sees it this solidarity serves as "a core of resistance to assimilation... and the need for change of lifeways is thus placed within a larger pattern of conduct and feeling, which serves better than the Puerto Rican pattern to ease the shock, to avoid the conflict in American society... In their struggle to escape a minority position, they can thus reach and borrow prestige from some larger and more favored minority."[2]

This emerging consciousness continued to grow during the early fifties to the point that when Elena Padilla published her study of Eastville *Up from Puerto Rico*, she uses "Hispanos" as the preferred way Puerto Ricans refer to themselves in New York. Eastville is El Barrio Latino, or Spanish Harlem. This has continued to be so to a large extent; however, certain factors have come to play on the situation, making the term "puertorriqueño" and a brand of "puertorriqueñismo" the desired term to be used when Puerto Ricans refer to themselves.

Among the trends that changed the situation was the development of the "hometown groups" in large numbers during the fifties to the point where they became one of the strongest influences in the organizational life of the community. Belonging to these groups meant a reaffirmation not only of one's place of birth but of being a Puerto Rican.

Another factor was the withdrawal of the Puerto Rican leadership from the *Desfile Hispano* and the organization of the annual Puerto Rican parade. Even though Puerto Rican groups still mingled and participated in the *Desfile*

Hispano, they merged shortly afterwards under the name of *Desfile Puertorriqueño*. The banners, the floats, the symbolic unity of the community was mostly Puerto Rican in character and origin; hispanic elements were secondary.

A third factor was the growth in population during the fifties and sixties, making the Puerto Rican community a potentially important political and economic portion of the life of the city. When looking at themselves Puerto Ricans slowly found themselves belonging to a community which was organizing itself and increasingly representing itself not as *Hispanos* but as Puerto Ricans.

Of no less importance were the changes in Puerto Rico during the fifties and sixties, from a poor underdeveloped area to a more industrialized, highly publicized, developing country. Puerto Rico became a great tourist attraction. More and more Americans, among them many New Yorkers, visited Puerto Rico and came back praising the beauty of the Island and the economic advances accomplished in a short span of years. Posters, films, and pamphlets announcing the gains were made circulate in both English and Spanish.

Many Puerto Ricans who had not been back to the island made a point of saving some money to go themselves and take their children to visit the Island. The slums they left were slowly disappearing and Santurce and San Juan became very cosmopolitan. The ease of transportation and cheap rates helped in the process of reacquainting many migrants with their country of origin, helping in the process to strengthen pride in their homeland.

The politicians on both sides, Puerto Ricans and Americans, saw the advantage of reorganizing this community politically, since Puerto Ricans, as citizens, could register and vote in large numbers, larger than those of other Latin Americans. There is always an advantage in the coalitions of Puerto Ricans with other Latin Americans, but there was no doubt that the political leadership slowly shifted from the *Hispanos* to Puerto Ricans.

With the advent of the poverty programs, it was mostly Puerto Ricans who were identified as the "poor"; the programs were directed to Puerto Ricans, and positions were given to them rather than to other Latin Americans.

There are always clubs and organizations that preserved their names as Hispanic societies, but most of the new groups formed by Puerto Ricans were called Puerto Rican groups.

Another term used by new groups which is even more nativistic is *Boricua*. It comes from the Indian name of the island of Puerto Rico, *Boriquen*. This is used by many Puerto Ricans, and especially by the Spanish press, as a symbol of the cultural identity of Puerto Ricans when it is reaffirmed *vis-a-vis* American culture. It has a great deal of acceptance, especially by militant and radical groups, as a symbol of the rejection of both Hispanic and American culture; however, it can be and is used by most elements in the community in the generalized context of nativism.

The second and third generation, and even the first generation who came here a long time ago, are at times referred to as Neo-Ricans, both in

New York and Puerto Rico. The term is a combination of "New York" and "Puerto Rican". It has found acceptance in writings and newspaper accounts, but apparently it has not yet challenged the brand of *puertorriqueñismo* or *Hispanismo* described so far. It is a term which has not yet been truly conceived and accepted by those to whom it applied. Some writers are using "Rican" as another way of referring to this group. Rican is seen in the graffiti of the subways next to the numbers of the streets where the writers of the graffiti live. It is a new term; it is hard to tell whether it will be commonly accepted in the future. It appears in private conversations but more commonly is used by the migrant himself who does not yet like it used by other people. This is a new development; it may be pointing to a new trend of assimilationist classification.

With the influx of large numbers of Cuban refugees the situation of the hispanic world in New York has become more complex. The Cuban groups in New York City have identified themselves culturally and politically with a conservative point of view. They reject as anti-American many of the ingredients of the cultural nationalism of Puerto Ricans, which they brand as political nationalism. The strain has been accentuated because Cubans came to New York City as refugees from Castro's regime during the sixties, when Puerto Rican militancy, radicalism and polarization of ideologies was at a peak both in New York and in Puerto Rico. On the surface, both groups participate in hispanic activities, but the cleavage is there ready to show itself on different occasions. The conservative elements in the Puerto Rican community have found allies in this Cuban group and in the elitist conservative elements of Latin America, who respond also to a class differentiation. These groups want little to do with the poorer elements in the migrant community and the communities of poor Latin Americans and are slowly emerging as a new force ready to protest any movement which may look socialistic or even too liberal. Being branded communists by this group is part of the experience of many people in the Puerto Rican and Latin American community who are far from subscribing to this partisan ideology.

As a result of this development Cuban refugees and other elitist Spaniards and Latin Americans together reorganized the *Desfile Hispano* into the *Desfile de la Raza*, which is celebrated during October, Discovery Day, and looks to the Consulates and dignitaries from Spain and Latin America as their true representatives.[5]

These groups do not look to the Puerto Rican mayors, who are popularly elected by the masses in Puerto Rico, as their representatives; and even though they send some groups to march in the Puerto Rican *Desfile*, they feel that theirs is the *Desfile* of the more refined elements in the Spanish speaking community.

The complication exists also when Cuban radical elements try to organize festivals of films, arts, or political meetings in the city. In March a film festival of Cuban-made films was interrupted and bomb threats were made to such a point that the festival could not be held. A recent conference of

Puerto Rican and other radical Latin Americans at Queens College was interrupted and acid was thrown at the faces of some of the participants.

When the Puerto Rican *Independentistas* got the Cuban delegate to present the case of Puerto Rico to the Committee on Decolonization of the United Nations, a Cuban faction was ready to march and stop the Puerto Rican meeting which was taking place in the UN Plaza.[7]

These confrontations will continue, with a resulting factionalism in the Hispanic community which always existed, but not to this extent, during the fifties and early sixties.

From the beginning of the Cuban influx, the Cubans, political anti-communist refugees, have obtained preferential treatment from the agencies of Federal Government, and to a certain extent, from the city and state governments. The U.S. Employment Service started services for the Cubans they never had for the Puerto Rican migrants. In many instances, Cubans are preferred over Puerto Ricans for positions with civic programs, giving rise to strife and competition which has added to ill feelings already created in the overall Hispanic community.[8]

This whole situation is aggravated by the influx of poor Dominicans in New York City. They are settling in the poorer sections of the city, alongside the poor Puerto Ricans. They are more radical in their demands for housing and social reforms, and their liberal leadership has joined Puerto Ricans in their struggle for equality and an end to discrimination. One of the areas already affected by this situation is the West Side of Manhattan, in the vicinity of Columbia University, where many Dominicans have joined Puerto Ricans in the "squatter movement" in housing.

This factionalism is not without a great deal of ambivalence. These groups, whether conservative, liberal, or radical, know that they have a difficult situation of adjustment in an Anglo-dominated culture, and in the last analysis, if the United States recognizes Cuba sometime in the future, the political refugee status of the Cubans will not hold. However, since most upper-class Cubans are white, the discrimination against them may be lesser than that directed toward the less privileged and darker-skinned elements in the Puerto Rican and Dominican communities.

The Puerto Rican politicians know that they must deal with this factionalism to build up a strong block of hispanic votes, which in a coalition with the Chicanos of the Northwest and Southwest could be a substantial block to use in bargaining with the principal parties.

There is one issue that unites all these factions so far; bilingual education. Chicanos, Puerto Ricans, Cubans and all Spanish speaking groups so far favor bilingual education. If they continue working on some mutually agreed-upon goals some measure of cooperation may be achieved in the future.[9]

In cultural and social affairs *Hispanos* meet on the basis of common interest and class identification. There are some organizations of poets, writers, and painters, and some organizations of a religious character which existed from the very beginning and which continue to function for common purposes. But for the present there is factionalism in the economic and political areas of the life of the community.

Looking in retrospect to what Mills and Padilla found and described, one could say that even though Puerto Ricans seek coalitions with other displaced Latin Americans and find solidarity in associating with them, recent trends have reinforced in the Puerto Rican migrants their *puertorriqueñismo* and they have found in it a more viable and congenial way of identification as a group. It is very difficult to predict, but there are already signs which may point to *hispanismo* as an identity more suitable for those who do not wish to completely assimilate into American culture, but would eventually like to dissociate themselves from the poor people and the darker-skinned people in the community. *Puertorriqueñismo* may be the identity sought for those who also refuse to assimilate, but would not feel welcomed by the hispanic elements, and may remain within this identity as a more comfortable one for themselves and their children.

FOOTNOTES

1. C. W. Mills and Associates. *The Puerto Rican Journey* (Harper and Brothers, New York, 1950), P.136.
2. Ibid., p.138.
3. Elena Padilla, *Up From Puerto Rico*, (Columbia University Press, New York, 1958), p.32.
4. *El Diario de Nueva York*, April 22, 1973, April 27, 1973. May 15, 1973.
5. *El Diario de Nueva York*, March 3, 1972.
6. *El Diario de Nueva York*, March 20, 1972 and March 27, 1972.
7. *El Diario de Nueva York*, August 17, 1972 and August 18, 1972.
8. *El Diario de Nueva York*, August 18, 1972.
9. Articles by Antonio Gil de Lamadrid. *Bilingual Education, a Priority in Education; El Diario de Nueva York*, March 7 and 8, 1972.
   [See also: Joseph P. Fitzpatrick, *Puerto Rican Americans* (Prentice Hall, Inc., Englewood Cliffs, New Jersey, 1971), pp.142]

CHAPTER IX
FINDINGS AND CONCLUSIONS

From the late nineteenth century, during the Spanish domination when Puerto Rican political parties were formally organized, the solution to the colonial status of the island was the central and predominant issue in politics. Party platforms have corresponded to the three central solutions to the status problem: independence, statehood and autonomy.

Social and economic reform programs were of secondary interest to the status issue, in spite of the poverty and underdevelopment of the island. After the elections of 1940, when the Popular Democratic Party won the First elections, the emphasis slowly shifted from the status as a major issue to a program of social and economic reforms and political autonomy as central to the political platform of the P.D.P.

Personalism and a policy of loyalty to the leader and his party are patterns which characterize the political participation of Puerto Ricans in Puerto Rico.

Centralization both in government and party structure are predominant characteristics of political institutions in Puerto Rico, with a tendency to have authority flowing from the leader of the party to the lower levels of the structure. There is a tendency to find solutions for problems in a strong personalistic fashion and to look up to the top of the pyramid of power for those solutions that are sought.

Dependence on a metropolitan power, first Spain, later the United States, is accepted as inevitable. Ways are found to deal with this reality without losing the illusion of more home rule for the Island. Challenges to this predominant centrist-reformist attitude come from elements at the two poles of the continuum: separation and integration, with periods of intense polarization followed by a return to the center and promises of reforms by island politicians.

Issues are very close to the lives of most citizens, and a high rate of voting is characteristic during elections. Politics is a way of life and it is deeply felt, argued, and discussed.

Even though parties are institutionalized, the structures are loose enough to allow for ease of participation. Coalitions of parties subscribing to different ideologies have been common in the past. A certain degree of pragmatism is allowed in the search for political power and victory at the polls.

With industrialization and urbanization, changes in these patterns are occurring, and a middle-class approach to politics is developing in the urban areas and the suburbs. Towns and *barrios* of the interior of the island, however, still cling to most of the traditional patterns of partisan participation.

Americans and "things American" are the object of a deep ambivalent feeling. There is a great admiration for the social and political institutions, but fear and distrust of American imperialism and expansionism. The American is emulated on the one hand, resisted on the other. A *modus vivendi* has been developed and these feelings are restrained and kept in abeyance.

A good politician has his own style, possesses verve and rhetoric, and delivers lengthy speeches in a grand manner. His personal life is closely followed, and even though Puerto Ricans have forgiven some of their politicians for their marital trespasses, they seldom forget and continue to keep a vigilant eye on their private lives.

Puerto Ricans are proud of their national culture, and even though there is a great penetration by the American culture, there is a desire to cling to things which are Puerto Rican. Political leaders are aware of this and know this is a theme that must be played if voters are to be attracted. Even statehood is asked with a "jibaro"* flavor. This illusion must be maintained at all costs.

When Puerto Ricans migrate, their cultural baggage includes some or all of the patterns described above. Other pattern will be developed with the experience of migration and the inter-action with the leaders and political institutions of New York City.

During the first migration period, the Inter-War Period, the settlements, particularly East Harlem, provided the migrants with a tightly knit community where they could mingle with their own people and find a sense of peoplehood similar to the one they left on the island. They started to establish themselves both socially and culturally in organizations and groups. Due to the recency of their arrival, the main issues central to the life of the migrant continued to be those which were central to political participation in Puerto Rico, particularly the nationalist solution to the status with a political separation from the United States. Their favorite politician was one who helped with the problems of adjustment, but who also had a personalistic approach to politics and who favored independence as a solution to the status problem.

Their ways of participating with parades, speeches, and Puerto Rican banners were all similar to the patterns of active political participation in Puerto Rico.

There was a group who followed the developments of the Civil War in Spain and who identified both with the Spanish and upper class Latin Americans on the basis of culture and social class.

Party loyalty was not as pronounced as it became in later decades, and even though the majority of Puerto Ricans preferred the Democratic Party, there were Republican candidates and enough followers to campaign and elect the first Puerto Rican Republican Assemblyman to Albany. The closeness of the neighborhood made it easy to find and belong to political clubhouses and to participate in the organization of apartment buildings as captains, so as to attract other Puerto Ricans to register and vote.

The number of those registering diminished — compared to registration in Puerto Rico — due to the literacy test; however, because of economic

---

* "jibaro" is the name commonly given to the Puerto Rican peasant.

selectivity,* those who were literate registered and started to count as a political bloc in the particular congressional district where they lived.

These factors contributed to the development of certain patterns of participation which were unique to this group of migrants who came before World War II. Since transportation was not as easy as during the second period (after World War II), a large number of Puerto Ricans who came to New York City remained there. The settlement had a character of its own which was typically Puerto Rican and Hispanic, making it easier for the migrants to accept the break with the Island. Even the war itself, making it impossible to travel, helped the settlers to find permanence in the new community where they lived.

There was dependence on leaders from the already established political groups since the migrants lacked the resources to organize politically. Their status as citizens, however, made them a potentially significant group in their district, and politicians tried to win their votes.

During the Inter-War Period, the Puerto Rican migrants who had settled in New York City were largely ignored by both the Washington and Puerto Rican governments. The New York City Puerto Rican community was left to fend for itself. Their organizations and leaders negotiated directly with the New York City administration, the State and Federal governments, and the City's political parties. All these functions, which had been carried on in a similar fashion by other ethnic groups who had come to the City, were performed by the Puerto Rican community during this early period.

Discrimination has been a factor in the adjustment of Puerto Ricans to the City from the very beginning. Particular targets were the Negro and intermediate Puerto Ricans. However, the smallness of their numbers and their identification with other Hispanic groups softened to a large extent the impact on this first group. Cultural nationalism and the opportunity to mix with their own people made life easier for those who could not avoid discrimination because of color.

During this period several Puerto Rican leaders emerged; none actually became the "leader" to whom they owed their loyalty. They crossed party lines to vote for the first Puerto Rican Assemblyman, but still they learned politics from the men who ran the machine and represented the district where they resided — Fiorello La Guardia, a Fusion mayor, and Vito Marcantonio, a congressman of the American Labor Party with leftist leanings.

The ideology of socialism and labor had penetrated the conciousness of Puerto Ricans deeper than one would have expected, and in their political behavior in Harlem they showed it by joining unions in large numbers, participating in labor strikes, following Marcantonio, and supporting the Loyalist cause in the Spanish Civil War. A brand of anticlericalism was present, possibly a remnant of the identification of the church with the power and authority of the government during the Spanish domination.

---

* The emigrants of this period had to have enough money to travel by boat.

When World War II broke, Puerto Ricans proclaimed their loyalty by forming associations to write to and try to keep morale high among the soldiers, showing a ready adaptation and adjustment to the new situation in which they found themselves.

With the end of World War II, the community steadily grew in size. The ease of transportation by plane and the pull of the economy of New York City attracted many migrants to the City.

Urban renewal and new construction affected the Puerto Rican settlements, and dispersion of the Puerto Rican migrants accelerated, making them the hardest-hit group in the dislocation brought about by the demolition of the old neighborhoods. Puerto Ricans depended more and more on public housing, where they were but a "quota" of the neighborhood, making it difficult for them to participate in organizations and community activities and to belong to political organizations and clubhouses. This situation retarded the involvement of Puerto Ricans in politics in some of the new neighborhoods they moved into, and made it more difficult for them to become a majority in any particular political district and so win elections and elect their representatives.

With the growth in the number of Puerto Ricans, new organizations and clubs were organized to serve the social and cultural needs of the migrants. These groups proliferated and entered into coalitions and federations, with a new leadership emerging which looked for help in their process of organization to the Migration Division of the Office of the Commonwealth of Puerto Rico and to Puerto Rico itself as a source for bringing more cohesion and participation among its members.

With the organization of the hometown groups, and later the Congress of Puerto Rican Hometown Groups, as powers in the community, the presidents and leaders of these clubs started a closer cooperation and communication with the individual towns in Puerto Rico, their mayors, and other local dignataries. They made a special effort to cooperate with Luis Muñoz Marín, who was the foremost political leader, not only as Governor of Puerto Rico, but as the leader of the Popular Democratic Party.

The New York City administration and politicians developed communication with the Migration Division, the Governor of Puerto Rico, and other Puerto Rican politicians as representatives of the migrants. Migration conferences seeking solutions created by migration, and visits to Puerto Rico were organized to learn about the migrants background on the island. The Migration Division and its supervisory personnel were sought after as the representatives of the community. Programs and projects of the government and private agencies were planned with the consultation and participation of the Division. A pattern of dependence on Puerto Rico, its government agencies and its leaders was established.

Slowly the Puerto Ricans took over the leadership of the parade, changing it from a Spanish and Hispanic parade to a Puerto Rican parade, with the Governor of Puerto Rico, the Mayoress of San Juan, and the Mayors of the towns of Puerto Rico as the central figures of the *Desfile*.

The Democratic Party in New York City and the Popular Democratic Party in Puerto Rico developed close ties. The Wagner administration was in power in New York, and the Muñoz administration was in power in Puerto Rico, a power that lasted during the fifties and the early sixties.

In spite of the growth in size of the community, the closeness of the leadership of the City with Puerto Rico and the proliferation of the leaders and organizations in the New York City Puerto Rican community, the number of Puerto Ricans registering and voting did not grow proportionately. The representation of Puerto Ricans as elected officials and the inroads of Puerto Ricans into the Democratic and Republican party was practically non-existent. No outstanding political leader emerged to unify and lead the community and to stimulate Puerto Ricans to participate more actively in politics.

The lack of a leader capable of effectively organizing Puerto Ricans to compete for political power in the City had the effect of developing an intense competition among those aspiring for positions in politics and in the civic life of the community. The organization of the first agencies was accompanied by a great deal of friction, fragmentation and internal factionalism. This intense internal dynamics drained a great deal of the energy that should have been channeled in the direction of competition with other groups for their share of power and for the recognition of the Puerto Rican group as an organized entity in the life of the City, fully capable of representing itself. Some of these aggressions were also directed toward the Migration Division, making it a scapegoat for every failure the community was experiencing.

Until the middle sixties the Puerto Rican community was looked at as an immigrant community, passively accepting their role until their turn would come, just as it had come to other groups in the history of the City. With the advent of the Anti-Poverty Programs the Puerto Ricans were at first by-passed by the City in favor of the Blacks, who were more vocal and militant in their demands nationally and locally, and who were resorting to a brand of Black Power in their search for compensation for their deprived status in the City.

In their struggle to get adequate representation in the political arena and to get adequate financial resources, Puerto Ricans have always competed with the Blacks, the other group which is the minority and is represented in large numbers among the poor. This struggle has been particularly acute in the control of community corporations, where Puerto Ricans have actively campaigned and have voted in large numbers to assume control of most of the corporations of the settlements in which they constitute a majority.

With a new administration when Lindsay became mayor, Puerto Rican leadership suffered a setback. Between Lindsay and the migrants, the old lines and communication ceased to exist. The leaders claimed Lindsay was not helping Puerto Ricans as much as he did the Blacks. More Blacks than Puerto Ricans were appointed to policy-making positions in his administration, and they outnumbered Puerto Ricans in the powerful Council Against Poverty, where the Puerto Ricans had never been able to get anything approaching equality of representation.

In 1967 Puerto Ricans rioted in East Harlem, and slowly their tactics started to change. They became aggressive in the 26 community corporations representing the poverty areas of the City, and started to compete with the Blacks for control of the corporations of those areas in which they lived.

With access to programs, jobs, and resources, Puerto Ricans took advantage of the poverty programs to set up structures they never had in the past, discovering and training a new layer of leadership to represent the community.

In the protection of their civil rights Puerto Ricans adopted a militant stance they never had practiced in the past, participating in protests, marches, sit-ins, occupying government buildings, and changing to a radical posture as a minority group.

The youth of the Puerto Rican community, in cooperation with the Black youth, participated in activities to get colleges to offer ethnic programs and to achieve a policy of Open Admissions at the City Colleges of New York City.

New militant and radical groups appeared, the most important being the Young Lords Party, the Puerto Rican counterpart of the Black Panthers. Even though they advocated independence for Puerto Rico, the Young Lords did not have formal ties with the Puerto Rican pro-independence parties. Their main targets were the "oppressive institutions" of the City, particularly hospitals, which according to them did not adequately serve the poor of the City. The Young Lords consistently challenged the reform-liberal elements of the Puerto Rican community, with such tactics as occupation of conferences, interruption of activities, and parading in the annual Puerto Rican parade, chanting anti-imperialist slogans.

Other militant groups were organized, such as the pro-political prisoners committees. When the Young Lords changed the character of their organization from a Party to a Workers Committee, these pro-political prisoners committees, followed some of the tactics of the Lords in advocating independence and opposing the liberal elements in the community in the representation of the migrant community. These groups kept closer ties with the representatives of the Puerto Rican pro-independence groups and with Puerto Rico than the Lords did.

Even though Puerto Ricans have identified themselves with other Spanish-speaking groups on the basis of language and cultural heritage, "puertorriqueñismo" continues to be the basis of identification for the migrants. The patterns of groups organization and activities developed since the middle fifties have reinforced the migrants' identity as Puerto Ricans. The emergence of the hometown groups as the most important community group started a trend that has recently been reinforced by political and economic developments, such as anti-poverty programs. The "boricua" term is also used to emphasize Puerto Rican cultural nationalism and nativism.

Political alliances are sought by Puerto Rican and Hispanic politicians for political purposes, such as the *Latino Caucus* of the Democratic Party — an alliance of Chicanos and Puerto Ricans.

In New York City the Hispanic world is faced with an ideological cleavage from the migration of political refugees from Cuba during the sixties. This groups clashes with the leftist liberals and radical elements of the Puerto Rican and other Spanish-speaking groups in their plans and aspirations for the overthrow of Castro, suspecting any movement that may deviate from their ideology of communistic tendencies. In their desire to attain their political goals the Cuban element may introduce some dissidence in the attempts to unify these groups. The conservative political refugees have allied themselves to groups with similar ideologies, organizing activities to counteract the radical elements in the community. Violence and confrontation tactics from both sides may result in further factionalism within the Hispanic world of New York.

The greatest concentration of Puerto Ricans during the seventies is in the borough of The Bronx. Puerto Ricans, city-wide, are close to a million in number. Puerto Ricans are not satisfied with the 1970 U.S. Census count; there are reasons to believe the Census undercounted Puerto Ricans. If the Puerto Ricans have been under-counted, they are at a decided disadvantage since the money supplied by government funds and programs for political purposes and for aids of the needy is allocated on a population basis.

Puerto Ricans are the poorest group in the City; they live in segregated and poor neighborhoods and depend in large numbers on welfare. This has contributed to a stigmatization of the group and to persistent discrimination in housing, employment, and education. The poverty programs made it possible for Puerto Ricans to organize agencies with enough resources to help the already-organized community groups with training and resources to assume a new kind of leadership and representation for the Puerto Rican community. New leaders have emerged. The leadership role once held by the Migration Division of the Commonwealth of Puerto Rico is now in the hands of this new group of leaders, and is centralized and flows predominantly from anti-poverty agencies. These leaders have control of the organization of the two outstanding community activities: the Annual Puerto Rican *Desfile* and the *Fiesta Folklórica*. These leaders have communication with Puerto Rico, and the Puerto Rican Governor and mayors are still the main attraction at the *Desfile*. But there is no longer an agency of the Government of Puerto Rico which outlines the policy and organizes and coordinates the activities. The present leaders are not only assuming these activities but also the leadership in the political life of the community.

The campaign and elections of 1972 marked a turning point in the participation of Puerto Ricans in partisan politics. A non-partisan Voting and Registration Campaign was organized, which succeeded in registering 200,000 new voters. The organization and leadership of this campaign was undertaken by the Puerto Rican Community Development Project, The Bronx Multi-Service Center, and other organizations, among them the Migration Division of the Commonwealth of Puerto Rico, which cooperates and participates but no longer assumes leadership. The chief political organizer and leader of this registration drive was Congressman Herman Badillo.

The Democratic National Convention helped the Puerto Rican political leadership to organize and served as a stimulus for the registration drive of 1972.

More Puerto Rican candidates than ever ran for office; this also helped in the increase of the numbers of Puerto Ricans who registered to vote.

Herman Badillo ran in the 1973 Democratic mayoralty campaign. The organization of the Badillo campaign and the leadership that Badillo gave Puerto Ricans has greatly contributed to increase the participation of Puerto Ricans in politics in New York City. In this mayoralty race Badillo emerged as "the leader" of Puerto Ricans. He reached all social classes in the Puerto Rican community, and in the process helped to further politicize the community. Badillo came out second in the June 4 primaries. Although he lost the June 26 runoff, the effect of the campaign had two positive aspects: (1) they came out of the primaries with a political leader, Herman Badillo, to unify the group; and (2) larger numbers than ever of Puerto Ricans registered to vote. This increase in registration makes the Puerto Rican bloc a potentially significant one in New York City politics.

In a city polarized by ethnic and racial differences the Puerto Rican group is in a difficult position. The election results were bitter; the tone of the campaign, with racism an overt and covert central issue, made it clearer than ever that the group is subjected to a great deal of prejudice and discrimination, and stands alone politically. It must organize in such a manner that it can use its increased voting power as a leverage for entering into coalitions and bargaining for position.

It is difficult to predict whether the unification gained in the 1973 campaign will continue. Even though Puerto Ricans in New York City have been able to develop structures that help them in their organization for political participation, they still need help in their campaigns. Since their campaign contributions are necessarily small, they cannot by themselves back up their candidates running for office and so compete efficiently with other political groups. The leaders still need financial help from well-to-do Puerto Ricans. In the mayoralty primaries, for example, Badillo, in spite of contributions from New York City Puerto Ricans and other political supporters, had to depend to a large extent on funds coming from Puerto Rico.

This need for funds presents a continuing pattern of dependence on the Island, which brings out ambivalent feelings on the part of community leaders, but must be accepted as the reality of the economic situation of the community.

This dependence, however, does not have the same character it had during the fifties, when the Migration Division of the Commonwealth of Puerto Rico was the community leaders' only resource in their task of organization for political representation. The new agencies developed with anti-poverty funds and private donations have given them organizations of their own, with Boards of Directors and supervisors and administrators selected by the community itself to assume representation on their behalf.

Factionalism exists in the community both within the leadership for representation and advancement, as well as being rooted in political ideology. The status continues to be the central issue for some groups who favor independence or statehood as solutions to the political situation of the island. However, these groups appear to be a minority; most community leaders are actively engaged in programs for the advancement of the migrant community. Their chief goal is to increase the political power of Puerto Ricans in the City so that they are adequately represented and to equip the community to participate in the political process.

The cleavage in the political ideology continues; the militant and radical elements, although a minority, are strongly represented among the young, the professionals, and educated Puerto Ricans. Any political leader who emerges will have to deal with these groups and try to reach accommodations with them from time to time when the situation demands it.

In their aspirations for coalitions with the other Spanish-speaking groups, the cleavage between the Cuban and the militant and leftist elements of the community will continue to play a part. However, the beginnings of a coalition with the Chicanos in the *Latino Caucus* within the Democratic Party already promises some grounds for optimism for this goal.

Even though most Puerto Ricans follow the issues of the island, more and more the migrants' interests are shifting to those issues and situations which directly affect the lives of the community in New York City. Without wishing to predict, we may safely say that due to the ease of travel, the political ties of the island and the United States, and the availability of information about the island through newspapers, radio and T.V., the Puerto Rican migrants, more than any group before, will keep close to the situation they left behind in their homeland. However, the very fact that they live in New York brings the issues and situations affecting their life in the city closer to the migrants than in their former life on the island.

As more Puerto Ricans vote and run for office, the patterns of participation of Puerto Ricans in New York City may come closer to the patterns of involvement which characterize the general population in New York City. As resources are developed and more Puerto Ricans enter the lower and middle classes, their political behavior and political institutions may resemble more and more those of the majority group. At present, however, this is not the case. If one is going to establish a degree of resemblance, one would have to say that the predominant patterns are closer to those developed in Puerto Rico. The Island, its government, and its representatives are factors in the political organization and participation of Puerto Ricans in New York City.

The power of Puerto Ricans in New York based on party politics still depends to a large extent on the kind of support received from the Island. Election results in Puerto Rico are decisive for New York Puerto Ricans. As New York Puerto Ricans become more powerful, they will try to influence the situation on the Island, and the interlinks between Puerto Rico and the mainland party politics deepen and become more complex.

APPENDIX I

DATA AND FIELD WORK PROCEDURE

Although there has been a great deal of speculation on the political participation of Puerto Ricans in New York City, no research has been done so far to answer the questions posed in this study. This study is a beginning of research toward, and understanding of, this aspect of the social organization of the community.

To be able to study the patterns of political participation it was necessary for me to research the question first in Puerto Rico, as a background to understanding the patterns in New York City. I used secondary sources to trace the historical background and the development of the patterns in the life of the migrants in Puerto Rico.

A second step in this project took me into another historical exploration — this one in New York City — of the first migration period of Puerto Ricans prior to World War II. Except for one study published in 1938, there is nothing written on the migration of this group, who settled before the main wave of migrants came to the city. For this period interviews with some of the early settlers who participated as leaders and organizers and active participants of those days had to be sought. I was fortunate in establishing communication and rapport with one of the most active members of the community, who gave me freely of her time, allowing me to tape-record the main aspects of the interview for two hours. She also gave me access to her archives and papers. This lady, Doña Josefina Silva de Cintrón, had copies of her journal, an account of the life of the community for twelve years, and clippings, letters, and other documents which validated her recollections about the community of those days.

Through this contact I made other contacts with leaders who pioneered the organization of the community of those days. They gave freely of their time and gave further information on the life of this largely forgotten community. I had to exercise my objectivity as a researcher so as not to devote too much time to this period of the history of the community. I can only excuse myself by declaring that the misconceptions about this period were so great that my scientific curiosity was aroused to explore aspects which had never been touched by any researcher so far. This chapter is a beginning to an historical reconstruction of the life of Puerto Ricans when they first settled in New York City. As part of my future task as a student of this community, I hope to expand this portion, and to stimulate others to undertake a similar course of study and analysis.

My interviews with the settlers of the first migration period followed a format which was open-ended and flexible, so as to allow those interviewed to refresh their memories of their early experiences when they first came to the city. I usually allowed some time before the taping of the interview to put them at ease and to start them thinking about this period of their lives. I had already done part of this in an initial telephone contact, and I asked to search trough their files and archives for papers, clippings or documents which could help me in reconstructing the events and activities they had engaged in.

Following are some of the questions which I asked during their interviews:

> Where did you first come to New York City?
> Where was your first place of settlement?
> Where did you work for the first time?
> How did you get this job? Did you know English?
> Had you participated in community activities in Puerto Rico?
> How did you become involved in social and community activities in the community?
> What clubs did you belong to?
> What was the life of the community like at that time?
> How did you become interested in politics?
> To what party did you belong?
> With what political club were you affiliated in New York City?
> How did Puerto Ricans participate in politics at that time?

As the interviews developed, the key questions elicited the life stories of those interviewed, who, in their own different ways, described the life of the community and explained their own involvement in it. I participated as little as possible to allow for a free flow of memories. I validated the information I received through newspaper clippings or documents, or the references other leaders made to each other.

These leaders are still active in some kind of participation in the life of the community. I also asked them questions about their present activities as related to the questions of the research problem.

Upon returning from the interviews I transcribed them and noted points for research, and contacts for future interviews. The names in this study are the real names of those interviewed, used with their own permission when the interview was conducted.

I followed the same procedure with the interviews of the post-war period. This period was easier to research because of the availability of sources and the willingness of the interviewees to give out information.

The familiarity with the life of the community was another factor which helped a great deal, but also I had to continuously check my objectivity to be sure I was grasping the social reality of the community.

Limiting the scope of the phenomena to be studied went hand in hand with limiting the activities of participating and observing, and of choosing those leaders who should be interviewed. My prior participation helped me in this aspect, but I also used the Spanish newspapers, particularly *El Diario de Nueva York*, to guide me.

Although this newspaper is run as a tabloid it covers the activities of the community comprehensively, and has columnists who have observed the situation for years, and who deserve to be taken as valuable sources in any conscientious study of the community. I read the paper daily, and clipped all news that had to do with organizational and political life of the community. I organized these clippings in historical sequence and used them as a valuable supplement to the interviews and observations gathered.

The English dailies were also followed, particularly on the development of the 1972 political campaign and the mayoralty primaries and runoff of 1973.

The political activities, particularly the voting and registration campaign of the leaders and the political organizations, were followed very closely for two purposes: to see how the campaign was launched and to study closely the patterns of participation of the organizers, their volunteers, and those who registered to vote.

I went to meetings, visited offices and interviewed the organizations' leaders.

The political campaign itself was too vast to follow. However, I paid close attention to those activities where the leader Herman Badillo was involved, to see how he was developing as the political representative of this minority, and to observe how the community was organizing itself for participation.

This aspect was supplemented through participant observation in a political club house in East Harlem, in a predominantly Puerto Rican neighborhood. Through participation in the registration campaign I met grassroot leaders who were involved in helping organize Puerto Ricans politically, at a neighborhood level. This gave me the opportunity to observe Puerto Ricans and their involvement with the political situation of their district, their leaders, and also their growing interest in the candidacy of Herman Badillo for Mayor. I was accepted as a volunteer, and in no way was I rejected because of the difference in my educational background. They looked at me as a representative of the leadership of the community who was willing to come to the ghetto and partake of their political activities. Whether, at this point, they may think that I am an aspiring politician is hard to tell. They tried to find out, and I explained that I wanted to know more about their organization to be able to write about it. No resistance was encountered. The experience of this participation helped me to further clarify my thoughts and to supplement information gathered through interviews and other sources of information. I had no formal interview except with the leader of the club.

The interrelationship of the main activities of the community, such as the annual parade, *Fiesta de San Juan*, and others is great. Most of the leaders are involved in both aspects, the civic and the political. These activities helped me in my observations of the patterns of participation and the structure of the organizations and institutions. The role of the militant and radical segments of the community was also observed during these activities.

I found it particularly helpful to make a case study analysis of one of the main activities of the community so as to be able to observe in detail the organization process, the participation of the leaders, and the interrelationship of the different organizations of the community. I did such an analysis on the Annual Puerto Rican Parade, commonly called The *Desfile*. I started with interviews of the founders of the Puerto Rican *Desfile* to inquire about their reasons for seceding from the Hispanic *Desfile*. These interviews were tape-recorded. I believe this is the first time this kind of research has been done, and that it will help in future research and historical reconstruction. I supplemented with documents, newspapers, and my own observation of the *Desfile*, the outstanding communal activity.

Following the progress of the *Desfile* in historical sequence, I found that it is a microcosm of the development of the community. The social forces affecting the new community, the new trends, conflicts, factionalism, growth, radicalization, and increasing politicizing process of the community — all could be observed in this in-depth analysis. This analysis clearly shows the ups and downs, the strength and weaknesses, of the Puerto Rican community. It was a detailed and difficult process, but it served to clarify and to clear up many of the findings of the research, which by themselves were difficult to understand.

Studying the radicalization of the community during the sixties required me to do a great deal of selectivity in the interviewing and in the selection of data to be included. In looking into the role of the Young Lords, I had gone to some of the activities for fund-raising purposes, demonstrations — such as the parade — and other functions where they had participated to explain their program. At this moment when I write, the group has changed its identity, but an interview in the summer of 1972 with a member of the group gave me a great deal of background information to include in my analysis.

Since the activities of the radical groups included civil rights militancy, I interviewed the leadership on this issue. On several occasions I interviewed and taped the controversial radical leader of the community, Gilberto Gerena Valentín. He is an articulate person, who, in addition to clarifying the radical position for me, gave me information and valuable insights into other aspects of the life of the community. As far as I could judge, he held back no information, helping me to refine my conceptions about the scope of the militant movement in New York. Since Gerena was the main organizer of the movement to stop the U.S. Civil Rights Hearings, I attended the hearings for several days to observe how he and other Puerto Ricans organized and carried out this activity.

These opportunities for first hand observation brought me into contact with the emerging cleavage between political factions within the Hispanic community, particularly between the Cuban refugees and the militant and radical Puerto Rican groups in the community. Conversely, I also observed this phenomenon by participating in the activities of some of the cultural groups who identify themselves with the Latin American elite, whose ideas are in consonance with a preservation of *status quo* governments in Central and South America. The entire spectrum of political groups was observed.

The trend toward a reaffirmation of *puertorriqueñismo vis-a-vis hispanismo* was the product of my observation of the development of the Puerto Rican community during the post-war migration period. Through interviews with Puerto Rican leaders I gathered this information. They gave me their impressions and helped me clarify what had initially been a hypothesis.

The data collection was non-systematic, as is necessary in and characteristic of historical studies.

SOURCES CONSULTED

Anderson, Robert. *Party Politics in Puerto Rico.* Stanford: Stanford University Press. 1965.

Arroyo, Angel M. *Taped Interview.* July 16, 1972.

Buckley, Tom. "Running for the Unrunnable", *The New York Times*, Sunday Magazine. June 3, 1973.

Chenault, Lawrence R. *The Puerto Rican Migrant In New York City.* New York: Columbia University Press. 1938. Re-issued, 1970. New York: Russell and Russell.

Clark, Victor S. and Associates. *Porto Rico and its Problems.* Washington, D.C. Brookings Institute. 1930.

Commonwealth of Puerto Rico. Migration Division of the Department of Labor pamphlets. *A Summary of Facts and Figures, 1964-65 edition.* New York, 1965.

Commonwealth of Puerto Rico. Ed. by the Office of the Commonwealth of Puerto Rico in Washington, D.C. 2nd edition. *Documents on the Constitutional History of Puerto Rico.* Washington, D.C. June 1964.

De Armas, Encarnación Padilla. *Taped Interview.* August 5, 1972.

De Cintrón, Josefina Silva. Editor. *Revista Artes y Letras.* Vol I and II. New York. 1933-45. *Taped Interview.* August 11, 1972. Private collection of papers and documents.

Díaz-Soler, Luis. *Historia de la Esclavitud Negra en Puerto Rico, 1493-1890.* Río Piedras: Ediciones de la Universidad de Puerto Rico, 1953.

Diffie, Bailey and Diffie. S.W. *Porto Rico — A Broken Pledge.* New York: The Vanguard Press, 1931.

El Diario de Nueva York. December 6, 1969. July 15, 1970. October 15, 1970. February 2, 9, 15, 18. March 3, 20, 27. July 14, 19. November 17. December 12, 1972. February 16. March 12. April 22, 27. May 15, 1973.

Fitzpatrick, Joseph P. *Puerto Rican Americans — The Meaning of Migration to the Mainland.* New Jersey: Prentice Hall, 1971.

Gerena-Valentín, Gilberto. *Taped Interview.* July 18, 1972.

Gil de Lemadrid, Antonio. *Bilingual Education, A Priority in Education.* Articles in El Diario de Nueva York. March, 7, and 8, 1972.

Glazer, Nathan, and Moynihan, Daniel P. *Beyond the Melting Pot.* Cambridge: The MIT Press. 1963. 2nd edition, 1970.

Goodsell, Charles I. *Administration of a Revolution.* Boston: Harvard University Press, 1965.

Gotsch, John Warren. *"Puerto Rican Leadership in New York."* Unpublished Master Thesis. Sociology Department. New York University, 1966.

Handlin, Oscar. *The Newcomers — Negroes and Puerto Ricans in a Changing Metropolis.* Boston: Harvard University Press, 1959.

Lewis, Gordon K. *Puerto Rico — Freedom and Power in the Caribbean.* New York: Harper Torchbooks, 1963.

Liga de Mujeres Votantes de Nueva York. *Datos Para Votantes — 1972.* October 26, 1972.

Lugo-Silva, Enrique. *The Tugwell Administration in Puerto Rico — 1941-46.* Río Piedras: University of Puerto Rico Press, 1955.
Maldonado Denis, Manuel. *Puerto Rico — A Socio-Historic Interpretation.* New York: Vintage Books, 1972.
Mann, Arthur. *La Guardia — a Fighter Against His Times.* Vol. I. New York: J. B. Lippincott, 1959.
Mathews, Thomas. *Puerto Rican Politics and the New Deal.* Gainesville: University of Florida Press. 1960. *Luis Muñoz Marín —A Concise Biography,* New York: Institute of Caribbean Studies Editions. Roberta Strauss Fuerbacht. American R.D M. Corporation. 1967.
Mills, C. Wright, Senior, Clarence and Goldsen, Rose. *The Puerto Rican Journey.* New York: Harper and Brothers. 1950. Re-issued, 1967, New York: Russell and Russell.
Nardelli, Eugene. *Personal Interview.* June 28, 1973.
New York City Human Resources Administration — Community Development Agency. *Proceedings of the Mayor's Puerto Rican Community Conference.* 1967.
Osuna, G. J. *Education in Puerto Rico.* New York: Teachers College, Columbia University Press, 1949.
Padilla, Elena. *Up From Puerto Rico.* New York: Columbia University Press, 1958.
Pagán, Bolívar. *Historia de los Partidos Politicos Puertorriqueños.* Vol. I and II. San Juan: Librería Campos. 1959.
Pedreira, Antonio S. *Insularismo.* San Juan: Biblioteca de Autores Puertorriqueños, 1957.
Pérez, Federico. *Personal Interview.* October 17, 1972.
Perloff, Harvey S. *Puerto Rico's Economic Future.* Chicago: University of Chicago Press, 1950.
Puerto Rican Community development Project. Pamphlet. *Summary of Programs Operated by the Puerto Rican Community Development Project.* New York, 1972.
Quintero, Luisa. *Marginalia Column.* El Diario de Nueva York. August 25, 1972.
Reeves, Richard. *Badillo: A Profile.* New York Magazine. April 10, 1973.
Rubenstein, Annette T. and Associates. *I Vote My Conscience — Debates, Speeches and Writings of Vito Marcantonio, 1935-1950.* New York: The Vito Marcantonio Memorial. 1956.
Ruiz, Ruperto. *Taped Interview.* August 8, 1972.
Sayre, Wallace S. and Kaufman, Herbert. *Governing New York City.* New York: Russell Sage Foundation. 1960.
Steward, Julian and Associates. *The People of Puerto Rico.* Urbana: University of Illinois, 1956.
The New York Times. August 16, October 15, December 6, 1969. July 15, October 15, 1970. March 22, 1971. February 15, March 6, September 9, October 2, 15, November 17, 1972. April 2, June 3, 1973.
Thomas, William I. Znaniecki Florian. *The Polish Peasant in Europe and America*

— *A Monograph of an Immigrant Group.* Vol. V. Boston: The Gorham Press, 1920.

Tracy, Phil. Article: *"The Browning of the NDC — From Here to Tammany Hall.* The Village Voice, March 8, 1973.

Tugwell, Rexford G. *The Stricken Land.* Garden City: Doubleday and Co, 1947.

United States Bureau of the Census. *Family Income of Spanish-Speaking Families in the United States.* Washington: Superintendent of Documents. No. 224, 1971.

Vivas, José Luis. *Historia de Puerto Rico.* New York: Las Americas Publishing House, 1962.

Wagenheim, Kal. *Puerto Rico: A Profile.* New York: Praeger Paperbacks, 1970.

Wakefield, Daniel, *Island in the City — The World of Spanish Harlem.* Boston: Houghton Mifflin Company, 1959.

Warner, W. Lloyd, Lunt, Paul S. *The Social Life of a Modern Community.* Vol I. New Haven: Yale University Press, 1941.